Mindfulness in a Busy World

Lowering Barriers for Adults and Youth to Cultivate Focus, Emotional Peace, and Gratefulness

Marie-Nathalie Beaudoin
Kelsey Maki

ROWMAN & LITTLEFIELD
Lanham • Boulder • New York • London

Executive Editor: Mark Kerr
Associate Editor: Courtney Packard
Production Editor: Lara Hahn
Cover Designer: Diana Nuhn

Credits and acknowledgments of sources for material or information used with permission appear on the appropriate page within the text.

Published by Rowman & Littlefield
An imprint of The Rowman & Littlefield Publishing Group, Inc.
4501 Forbes Boulevard, Suite 200, Lanham, Maryland 20706
www.rowman.com

6 Tinworth Street, London, SE11 5AL, United Kingdom

British Library Cataloguing in Publication Information Available

Library of Congress Cataloging-in-Publication Data Available
ISBN 978-1-5381-3512-9 (cloth : alk. paper)
ISBN 978-1-5381-3513-6 (pbk. : alk. paper)
ISBN 978-1-5381-3514-3 (ebook)

∞™ The paper used in this publication meets the minimum requirements of American National Standard for Information Sciences—Permanence of Paper for Printed Library Materials, ANSI/NISO Z39.48–1992.

To all the beautiful people shimmering under the weight of busyness,
To my thoughtful children, who keep me intrigued by life,
To my loving husband, whose interest in my ideas keeps them coming.

—Marie-Nathalie Beaudoin

To all the people who have supported me in this journey—my husband, family, friends, and supervisors—I would not be where I am today without your encouragement and guidance.

—Kelsey Maki

In the midst of winter,
I finally learned,
That there was in me,
An invincible summer.

—Albert Camus

Contents

PREFACE

~

How This Book Came into Existence

When people sought therapy for anxiety, stress, and self-doubt in the 1990s, and I (MNB) asked them if they had heard of mindfulness, they would invariably answer, "No, what's that?" and I could expose them to some appeasing practices, and refer them to what had been, for me, a life-changing mindfulness-based stress reduction program (MBSR). Now, 30 years later, my practice is filled with even more people struggling with these issues, but when I ask the same question, people reply, "Oh! Yeah! I've tried that; it doesn't work for me," followed by explanations such as "Honestly, I found it boring," or "I like to think all the time; I really have no desire to stop," or "My mind was wandering the whole time the instructor was talking, so it was a total waste of my time." While therapy alone, such as narrative and collaborative approaches, can help people tremendously with reducing anxiety and other struggles, having access to mindfulness practices can often accelerate the process and allow them to discover other ways of being.

During the same period of time, I also witnessed a shift in the education world. In the 1990s, I was training and supervising counselors for 13 schools, and most referrals were about conflicts with peers, families, teachers, and bullying. Rather than offering the typical anti-bullying project, I approached the issue from a different angle: if we increased mindful self-awareness, compassion toward others, and strictly gave attention to children's small daily moments of effort (i.e., "when they tried to keep a problem small"), shouldn't problems reduce? Research on the brain clearly shows that giving attention to what we do well usually allows us to better repeat it. This approach ended up being very successful, way beyond what we expected, and levels of empathy skyrocketed when compared to control groups (Beaudoin, 2010, 2014; Beaudoin, Moersch, & Schnare, 2016; Beaudoin & Taylor, 2009). While these meaningful and thoughtful projects are still popular and help improve socio-emotional skills, the referrals have now somewhat evolved. Teachers and parents are increasingly seeking help for students struggling with not listening, not paying attention, forgetting, impulsivity, inability to calm down, and lack of awareness.

The combination of these observations in private practice and schools has led me to focus on developing mindfulness projects and breathing exercises to address these alarming issues. People become who they practice to be, so let us give them compelling opportunities to discover in themselves, and experience firsthand, the little-known capacities of their minds. You can only fully realize a potential you know you have.

In 2017–2019, two wonderful developments happened. Kelsey came along to SKIPS, with her beautiful writing style, her research interest, and her own creative ideas. She became a superstar in schools, facilitating the projects with grace, and both children and adults adored her gentle ways. A few months later, Rowman & Littlefield contacted me about publishing a book on mindfulness, and I was delighted that Kelsey agreed to do this with me. This became a lovely journey of teamwork with Mark Kerr, our editor extraordinaire, and Courtney Packard, his super helpful editorial assistant.

We hope you will enjoy the innovative exercises presented in this book, and that they will take you and your participants a step closer to embodied experiences of calm, focus, kindness, belonging, and gratitude.

—Marie-Nathalie Beaudoin

Acknowledgments

We would like to thank our editor, Mark Kerr, for his enthusiasm about this book, and for his vision of helping educators and psychologists incorporate engaging mindfulness practices in their work. We also greatly appreciate Courtney's diligent replies to our quick questions and her helpful tips as we navigated illustration edits and final steps.

Marie-Nathalie would like to express her profound gratitude to the many mindfulness and yoga teachers who have inspired her along the way: Patrick Thornton, who first introduced these ideas in the 1990s in the Mindfulness-Based Stress Reduction program directed by Bob Stahl at El Camino Hospital, and who was an outstanding teacher, balancing big-picture concepts with intricate details; Jack Kornfield; Jon Kabat-Zinn; Myla Kabat-Zinn; Debra Chamberlain; Rick Hanson; Tara Bracht; and many others who were so remarkably skilled at creating beautiful, evocative, and haunting experiences, facilitating a keen observation of what is taken for granted and an openness to what is possible; the Dalai Lama and Thupten Jinpa, who have a graceful way of combining important questions and considerations with humor; and local wise people such as Bintu Coleman, Jonathan Han, Joanie Cartal, Doris Palmer, Lynn Anderson, and, in particular, John Dennery, whose depth of experience with gentle therapeutic yoga and mindfulness seems to have no end.

Kelsey would first and foremost like to thank Marie-Nathalie, whose patient supervision, positive encouragement, and inventive therapeutic methods made the exploration of these mindfulness experiences possible. Dr. Marie, thank you so much for inviting me to share in this work—your unwavering trust allowed me to believe in myself as a clinician and a writer, and your creativity was a constant inspiration throughout this project.

We would also like to acknowledge our adult clients, who have been open to these ideas even though they might not have believed in their value at first; the young people in schools who have been so willing to participate in these projects and give us feedback; the principals and teachers who have invited us into their classrooms and shared their views; workshop participants from all over the world who gave some of their precious time to hear, learn, and experiment with some of these practices; the doctoral interns at SKIPS who experimented with facilitating these programs; and, in particular, Michelle Renwick, who, with her kind and charming presence, made several valuable recommendations to tweak some wordings. Of course, none of this work would have been possible without the invisible support of our loving families, who, behind the scenes, took care of so many things! For Marie-Nathalie, this includes Paul, Esther, Meika, and Emilie. For Kelsey, this involves Richard, Susan, Dave, Jonah, and Ben.

Introduction

In 2005, a scientific earthquake shook the world: mindfulness meditation, previously practiced mostly in Eastern countries, was found to undeniably alter *physiological structures* of the brain! Scientists from all over the world rushed to replicate this unbelievable Harvard study (Lazar et al., 2005) and to investigate in depth how mindfulness can actually change a person's brain. Strings of results were published, and walls around disciplines temporarily shattered as mindfulness was applied, studied, and taught in a myriad of fields to medical students, athletes, business professionals, artists, trauma victims, pain patients, anxiety sufferers, older adults, teachers, parents, etc. Everyone with a personal struggle, or with enough time on their hands to explore this unique experience, rushed to the table to experience mindfulness' numerous benefits. While many people tried mindfulness meditation, some gave up the practice too early without having fully experienced the depth of its advantages. Why? Because their minds are trapped in a habit of overthinking certain subjects and under-focusing on others, which can playfully be coined as "thinkitis" (Beaudoin, 2018). This habit is difficult to break. Traditional mindfulness practices may not be readily within reach of people captured by a busy lifestyle involving constant mental churning, an emphasis on doing rather than being, and the constant stimulations of the modern world.

In some subcultures in the West, busyness has even become a status symbol—people who are busier and have less leisure time are considered more ambitious and competent (Bellezza, Paharia, & Keinan, 2017). The use of media and multitasking through media seems to have increased this sense of busyness. Now that we have smartphones with multiple capabilities, we can continue to receive work emails or messages long after leaving the office. The availability of smartphones and other electronics has also brought an increase in multitasking, particularly with different kinds of media. Both youth and adults experience an endless flow of emails flashing on their computer screens while they are working, frequent dings of texts coming in during conversations, and the background noise of TV, music, or YouTube videos while they are reading an internet article. When using their smartphones, people switch to a different screen or app every 20 seconds on average, and rarely spend more than 20 uninterrupted minutes on a single media activity, even a full-length movie (Carey, 2019). This constant switching back and forth to different screens and activities throughout the day is known as "media multitasking." Although a small group of the population can multitask effectively, in approximately 90% of people the brain is not built for multitasking. The vast majority of people experience a decrease in their work productivity and quality when multitasking (Chow, 2013). Because of the brain's neuroplasticity, and its amazing ability to shift and reorganize, chronic media multitasking can actually *change* the brain in an alarming way—those who engage in frequent media multitasking tend to have smaller anterior cingulate cortices (Loh & Kanai, 2014), an area of the brain involved in both emotion regulation and cognitive control.

These brain changes are reflected in the everyday life of media multitaskers—they may experience increased attention difficulties (Shin, Webb, & Kemps, 2019) and decreased academic or work achievement (Martín-Perpiña, Poch, & Cerrato, 2019), as it becomes more difficult to focus on class or work assignments. Heavy media multitasking is also correlated with depression, social anxiety, and difficulty sleeping (van der Schuur, Baumgartner, Sumter, & Valkenberg, 2015). Unfortunately, once media multitasking becomes a habit, it is difficult to break. Our darting minds and tendency to switch tasks can make it difficult to be present in meaningful ways in relationships, work, and everyday tasks. We are constantly looking toward the *next* thing that will bring true happiness, and therefore struggle to find joy in the present moment (Harris, 2014). This is exactly why mindfulness practices are so crucial at this time in our history.

Yet introducing mindfulness meditation in work settings or schools, where people are already tired from long hours spent sitting, can seem daunting. Moreover, some people are not comfortable with internal focus, as it is often associated with self-doubt, self-blame, and self-scrutiny. Many of the people who would most benefit from mindfulness experiences are often the least able to sustain it. This creates an important dilemma: we have a powerful method to increase concentration, focus, patience, inner peace, and kindness, and we know people in our modern world are in dire need of learning these skills, and yet the people who most need it have a lesser likelihood of sustaining these practices. How can the method benefit those who most need it? By tapping into a whole other body of research on attention circuits in the brain. Scholars have conducted a great deal of research on the brain's tendency to increase attention to situations involving, for example, novelty, fears, gains, and personal meaning. Combining knowledge from mindfulness and neurobiology along with practical clinical experience, this book bridges that gap by offering mindfulness exercises that engage everyone through the recruitment of attention circuits in the brain. Most of the mindfulness meditation exercises in this book are completely novel and creative, while others infuse ancient, well-loved practices (such as the body scan or mountain meditation) with intriguing and scientific setups that increase people's abilities to pay attention and reap benefits.

The concept of mindfulness meditation "exercises" may feel like an oxymoron to the experienced practitioner. Mindfulness is known to encourage *being* rather than *doing*. Mindfulness focuses on *experiences*, not *tasks*. Mindfulness encourages perspective and observation in the *present* time, rather than *factual* knowledge and *future* outcomes. How can the words "exercise" and "facts" coexist with mindfulness meditation? These components lie in the setup, context, and stage upon which people become intrigued by the experience and *more interested to try it right then and there*. They mobilize what draws people's attention: questions, mysteries, intrigue, and discomfort. Once mobilized, curiosity paves the way to entering the world of observation, peace, focus, and kindness.

Mindfulness meditation allows people to experience greater competency over their thoughts, emotions, health, pain, and even relationships. The projects in this book help people discover these important benefits and become in awe of their own minds by exposing them to simple but fascinating tasks that can be accomplished only through mindfulness. Participants become captivated by their discoveries, look forward to the projects, and are more likely to take up the practice at home. The facilitation transcripts are written to accommodate groups of adults or young people, with specific directions included for each population.

What This Book Is Not

A One-Size-Fits-All Approach

This book was written as a response to the busy, on-the-go Western culture, particularly in the United States, where these exercises have been developed. Many of these practices are meant to scaffold a mindfulness experience for people who are immersed in a culture of video gaming, multitasking, or overthinking. The exercises that we have created often start with factual information to hook the overthinking mind into being curious. Once thinking is mobilized to be curious about present time experience, then we transition into states of present time observation and sensing, a mindfulness state. We feel that this allows more people to put in the effort of taming their minds.

For cultures or communities of people who are already acutely present to their lives, these exercises might actually have the opposite effect. If people are living fully in the "now" (Tolle, 2004), are keen observers, and are mostly connected to their senses and embodied experiences, providing them with lots of information and exercises might actually take them away from mindfulness in the here and now. For these people, the eight-week Mindfulness-Based Stress Reduction (MBSR) program or a traditional, month-long, silent Vipassana retreat may be more conducive to enhancing their mindfulness.

A Quick Set of Techniques

Mindfulness is a rich Eastern tradition, anchored in thousands of years of wisdom and teachings. Since its introduction in the West, it has been receiving a growing amount of attention, some of which is inappropriate. In some circles, it is unfortunately becoming the new promise of a quick fix, or a checkmark on a list of fashionable things to try. I (MNB) was once attending a seminar from his Holiness the Dalai Lama, and when he offered the possibility of asking questions, a man stood up to ask what was "the quickest way to enlightenment"! There was a murmur in the audience. His Holiness smiled and kindly replied that there is none; it is a journey, it is not about getting quickly to an outcome!

Our fast-paced, capitalistic world is obsessed with glimmering gains, measurable outcomes, rewards, monetary success, and the future. In this endeavor, much is lost. The excessive focus on future outcomes skews many of our experiences. Real life is zooming by with every minute of our mind's attempt at controlling an imagined future or calculating what we'll gain (or lose) if we do x, y, or z. This is well illustrated by the following contemporary story (in Feldman & Kornfield, 1991, p. 306):

> The rich industrialist from the North was horrified to find the Southern fisherman lying lazily beside his boat, smoking a pipe. "Why aren't you out fishing?" said the industrialist. "Because I have caught enough fish for the day," said the fisherman.
>
> "Why don't you catch some more?"

"What would I do with it?"

"You could earn more money" was the reply. "With that you could have a motor fixed to your boat to go into deeper waters and catch more fish. ... Then you'd be a rich man like me."

"What would I do then?"

"Then you could really enjoy life."

"What do you think I'm doing right now?"

Realistically, we all have to be involved in working, studying, fulfilling our responsibilities, and trying to earn a living. We also wish to raise children who are hardworking and willing to put their best effort into their tasks. The issue arises when productivity and thinking become overly prized and systematically erase the possibilities of just *being* in the unfolding moment in which we are immersed. Many people no longer experience mindful pauses in their lives, such as the quiet of driving back from work in silence (without music), being engrossed in the colors of the sunset (without taking a photo), waking up in the morning to the sounds of birds (without the radio), or eating as a family engaged in discussions (without television).

Mindfulness is about being more centered in the rich present time, enjoyment, letting go, being kind, focusing with curiosity, and sensing what is. It is about silencing the constant noise of the chattering mind that is overanalyzing the past or the future and judging ourselves and others. Mindfulness can lead to enjoying a more fulfilling life, attaining higher states of awareness, or freeing ourselves/others from struggles. Yet it must also be embedded in "noble truths," values, awareness, presence, and gratefulness. The exercises featured in this book render powerful traditions visible and accessible. Please teach them with kindness, patience, compassion, and respect. Our intention, in sharing these practices, is to help more people tap into budding, precious skills that may otherwise not have the opportunity to blossom in the context of a busy, distracted lifestyle.

Overview of This Book

This book is divided into eight chapters. The first chapter provides a theoretical backdrop with an introduction to the many remarkable benefits of mindfulness. The second chapter offers important facilitation tips, and the third summarizes fascinating brain research on the process of engaging and sustaining people's attention. The remaining chapters include a variety of special mindfulness exercises that progressively increase participants' levels of focusing and regulation skills. The fourth chapter introduces a foundational skill of mindfulness—breathing—and includes 18 powerful exercises to help people better manage their emotions and biologically reset their bodies when overly agitated or stressed. The fifth chapter describes a wide range of mindfulness activities exploring the world of senses and culminating in people's increased personal trust, confidence, and mastery in the face of painful experiences. The sixth chapter increases participants' awareness of the science and sensations associated with several of their fascinating body parts. The seventh chapter describes belonging and gratefulness mindfulness meditations, which help people become aware of interconnectedness. The last chapter describes the Lord of the Rings project, where people become fascinated by their power to change their own hand's temperature and the color of a mood ring, biodot, or other biofeedback device. All chapters conclude with an intriguing challenge where participants are given the opportunity of testing their newly developed skills. These tests add a lot of excitement and make visible everyone's increased abilities to focus, remain calm, and sustain inner peace regardless of what happens around them. Above all, these tests allow participants to "graduate" with a heightened level of self-confidence and a sense of personal growth.

In sum, each chapter offers a description of unique and captivating exercises that can be used to develop many self-regulating and focusing skills and create greater group cohesiveness. They can also contribute to addressing problems such as anger management, anxiety, impulsivity, and concentration issues, or just for the cultivation of a peaceful mind. For the most part, they can be facilitated anytime and anywhere. Many work settings and educational environments find that it is well worth spending time increasing their employees' or students' self-awareness and emotional skills, since peaceful people of all ages are then better able to focus and perform.

We hope you will enjoy the new world of possibilities that unfold in the following pages.

CHAPTER ONE

Why Mindfulness Is Definitely Worth It at This Time in Our History

What Is Mindfulness?

Mindfulness is the art of intentionally focusing the mind on the present and being fully engaged with an object or experience. Most busy people, without training, cannot focus 100% of their mind on the sound of their breath or on the sensation of air flowing in and out of their body for even 30 seconds without allowing thoughts to distract them from their observation. We are steeped in a culture of electronic stimulation, multitasking, and busyness, constantly shifting between tasks (see Figure 1.1). Carey (2019) reports that smartphone users switch to a different screen or app every 20 seconds on average! For the overwhelming majority of people, this rate of multitasking is not compatible with how our brain is built to work. Even in young people—who may insist they can listen to music, watch a movie, and do their homework at the same time—media multitasking is associated with decreased academic achievement (Martín-Perpiña et al., 2019). In class, young people's minds are often flicking between listening to a teacher, replaying a video game, or reliving a conflict that took place at home. Because our brain is adaptable, its structure changes in unfortunate ways to get used to this pace, particularly areas responsible for regulating our thoughts and emotions (Loh & Kanai, 2014). Imagine how powerful and peaceful everyone could become if minds became fully controlled by their owners and didn't get stuck in repetitive and unproductive thinking!

Figure 1.1. The Human Brain Is Not as Well Equipped as Other Creatures to Successfully Multitask!

The ability to be mindful is developed by a number of practices, exercises, and lessons associated with complex traditions and teachings (Kabat-Zinn, 1990; Stahl & Goldstein, 2010). Over time, mindfulness becomes much more than a simple exercise of the mind to attain certain benefits. It is a philosophy of life, a grounded and expanded way of being, and an experience of the world mediated by openness, inner peace, kindness, compassion, and presence (see Figure 1.2) (Germer, 2014; Shapiro & Carlston, 2010). Studies with thousands of participants have shown over and over again that most people who successfully participate in an 8-week mindfulness program experience a new outlook on their lives. Even after years, many of them still incorporate some form of mindfulness in their lives, though they may not engage in its regular, disciplined practice. Not many "teachings" in our world can be marketed as having such transformative and long-lasting positive effects on most people's lives, regardless of age, gender, ethnicity, or personal struggles (Hanson & Medius, 2009).

Where Does the Practice of Mindfulness Meditation Come From?

The practice of mindfulness meditation is one of the many mind-mastery skills developed in centuries-old Buddhist traditions, but it does not require ties to the religion itself. It is taught in Buddhist theology but also exists in the secular environment, just as having strong values for "respect" is taught in both lay and religion-affiliated communities. Mindfulness was popularized in the United States by Jon Kabat-Zinn, who later developed his impressive stress reduction program at the University of Massachussetts Medical School in the early 1990s. Hundreds of other authors have also contributed immensely to increasing mindfulness' popularity and accessibility to the general public.

What Are the Benefits of Mindfulness?

Benefits for Brain Functioning and Cognition

Mindfulness training is proven to have benefits for a form of cognition known as executive functioning. *Executive functioning* (EF) is a term used in the field of psychology to describe the ability to direct attention, hold information, consider alternatives, prioritize, and plan. It is also crucial for novel problem solving, thinking "outside the box," and seeing events or facts from someone else's perspective (Diamond, 2013). These skills are generally housed within the prefrontal cortex of the brain, which, like the executive of a company, oversees and coordinates work among the other brain systems. We likely would not be able to make it through the day without using our EF—it is working constantly to help us plan and make thoughtful decisions in a way we often take for granted. For example, setting an alarm for the next morning before going to bed may feel like a simple and straightforward task, but it requires a great deal of higher-order functioning. Knowing what time to set your alarm for requires the engagement of your EF system to hold upcoming commitments in your mind, consider how much time you will need to get ready, and work backward to plan what time you need to wake up. In the morning, when that alarm goes off, your body may fight for a few extra minutes or hours of sleep. Your EF system may kick in to remind you of the consequences of waking up late, or it might help you figure out what you can cut out of your morning routine after you press the snooze button.

Even short-term mindfulness training can be beneficial for improving EF. After just four mindfulness meditation sessions, college students demonstrated a significant improvement in their working memory, attention span, and ability to process visual information efficiently (Zeidan, Johnson, Diamond, David, & Goolkasian, 2010). The working memory system holds information in the mind and mentally manipulates it—as you read this book, your working memory retains what your eyes perceive and the semantic knowledge it triggers in order to string words into meaningful sentences. Long-term pursuit of mindfulness practice is associated with continued improvements in EF and memory. Those who regularly practice mindfulness meditation have better short-term and long-

Figure 1.2. Mindfulness Practices Cultivate Many Aspects of Well-being and Connectedness.

term memory than their peers, and demonstrate increased preservation of problem-solving skills as they age (Gard et al., 2014).

Underlying these improvements in cognition and EF are lasting changes in the structure of the brain. Engaging in mindfulness meditation for just 8 weeks is associated with increased gray matter, particularly in brainstem areas associated with the release of neurotransmitters that impact attention, arousal, sleep, and mood (Singleton et al., 2014). Long-term mindfulness meditation is associated with increased gray matter in the hippocampus, a brain structure associated with memory, and the cerebellum, the area at the back of the brain linked with balance, posture, and coordinating muscle movements (Hölzel et al., 2011). Mindfulness meditators also have thickened grey matter in the prefrontal cortex (the CEO mentioned earlier) as well as the right anterior insula and temporal–parietal junction, areas associated with sensory processing and awareness of internal organs (Lazar et al., 2005).

The effects of mindfulness meditation on the brain are long lasting and can even protect against the cognitive decline that occurs with normal aging, such as a reduction in brain volume and weakened processing speed, problem solving, and memory. Older adults who were longtime mindfulness meditators showed more resilience to aging—they were less affected by damaging brain lesions or neuron aging than their non-meditating peers, and

Box 1.1 Mindfulness in Action

If you make mindfulness meditation a part of your daily routine, you may be able to turn back time when it comes to your brain. To examine just how much mindfulness meditation slows brain aging, researchers at the University of California–Los Angeles compared the brains of long-term meditation practitioners with same-aged non-meditation practitioners using neuroimaging technology. At age 50, the long-term meditators' brains looked about 7.5 years younger than their actual age. The gap between chronological age and brain age widens with continued mindfulness practice. In fact, for every year over 50, the brain looked an additional 1 month and 22 days younger on average. In theory, this means that you could celebrate your 80th birthday with a brain that does not look a day over 69 years old (Luders, Cherbuin, & Gaser, 2016).

they demonstrated a slower decline in their ability to solve novel problems (Gard et al., 2014). This has implications not only for those experiencing normal aging but also for people with serious neurocognitive impairment or dementia. For example, mindfulness interventions can reduce the rate of cognitive decline and brain volume loss even in those with Alzheimer's disease (Russell-Williams et al., 2018).

Heightened Self-Awareness

Although people often believe that they move through the world as impartial, objective beings, psychological research has demonstrated that this is not the case. In order to quickly make sense of the overwhelming amount of stimulation the world provides, the brain has come up with shortcuts that rely on previous experiences and emotional associations. These shortcuts color the ways people perceive events, and potentially lead to biases due to overlooked facts or false assumptions (Fiske, 2018). Mindfulness practices can help to reduce these biases in our perceptions, thoughts, and feelings by developing self-awareness.

In order to understand how mindfulness practices accomplish this, it is important to know what kind of "self" we are referring to. As we go about our daily lives, we have a "voice" in our brain narrating our experience, which is referred to as the *narrative self*. Many different forms of narrative selves can exist (White & Epston, 1990). They are often understood as thinking habits shaped by life experiences and sociocultural norms. The narrative self evaluates and reflects on experiences, notices some actions more than others, and makes judgments accordingly. If it is a negative narrative self, which can feel like an inner critic, it might berate us for saying something silly and then remind us of other embarrassing moments we have experienced. On its worst behavior, it can turn one isolated mistake into the global self-judgment of "I'm a failure." The dominant narrative self is influenced by biases from our brain and our culture, and therefore often leaves out information that might lead us to a different conclusion. In fact, an overactive narrative self can be associated with excessive and repetitive rumination, as well as decreased attention and capacity for information processing. In short, if given too long a leash, the voice in our heads can get us to be more in our thoughts than in our unfolding life, which can have negative health outcomes (Vago & Silbersweig, 2012).

A dominant narrative self also turns our stream-of-consciousness thoughts, judgments, and observations into a story about what kind of person we are. It interprets experiences in order to find adjectives that can become a part of our self-identity. For example, if we get a perfect score on an exam, this narrative self might tell us that we are "smart." If we continually have trouble getting along with others, and ascribe meaning to this, a problematic narrative self might decide that we are "awkward" or "unlikeable." For children, the reactions of teachers, peers, and family members contribute to the foundation of a dominant narrative about their identity (White, 2007). Children who have behavioral issues may develop the ideas that they are a "troublemaker" or "bad at school," which can have lasting consequences for the way they engage in learning and relationships.

Mindfulness meditation practices help people quiet the automatic assumptions, judgments, and self-attributions of the dominant narrative self, and therefore promote self-awareness. For example, after completing school-based awareness or mindfulness programs, children with behavioral issues demonstrated a shift in their self-identity, viewing themselves in a more positive light and with more self-compassion (Beaudoin, Moersch, & Schnare, 2016). Brain imaging research demonstrates that during mindfulness meditation, the language and emotion centers of the brain are less active, which likely means fewer internal verbalizations or emotional reactions during meditation (Lutz, Brühl, Scheerer, Jäncke, & Herwig, 2016). Our evaluative narrative self is quieted, which allows a deeper connection to the body and the present moment. Long-term meditators have less reactions to self-critical phrases and demonstrate more awareness, identification, and processing of their emotional states (Lutz et al., 2016). Instead of allowing the dominant narrative self to interpret emotional reactions as facts, mindfulness meditators can decenter themselves, meaning they view thoughts and feelings as temporary states not inherently related to the self (Fissler et al., 2016).

Improved Response to Stress and Emotion Regulation

Mindfulness practices have positive implications for the experience of emotions and stress. Those who practice mindfulness report experiencing less negative and more positive emotions even during times of stress and vulnerability, such as military pre-deployment (Jha, Stanley, Kiyonaga, Wong, & Gelfand, 2010) or pregnancy (Dhillon, Sparkes, & Duarte, 2017). Mindfulness practices help to reduce stress not by changing the circumstances of life, but by changing a person's relationship to stress. In women with breast cancer—a physically and psychologically daunting experience—mindfulness interventions reduced stress levels and improved reported quality of life (Monti et al., 2013). Research demonstrates that mindfulness meditation changes not only the reported feeling but also the physiological indicators of stress. When the body is under stress, the brain releases a hormone called cortisol, which gets the body ready for a "fight-or-flight" response by increasing blood pressure, shutting down digestion, increasing blood sugar levels, and suppressing the immune system. These effects are advantageous in the case of an actually life-threatening situation, but are not as helpful for everyday life. The impact of cortisol can even be harmful in the case of chronic stress. Mindfulness meditation can result in a drop in cortisol levels immediately after a session, protecting the body from these sorts of overreactions (Miodrag, Lense, & Dykens, 2013).

Reducing stress requires emotion regulation, which is the ability to effectively respond, manage, or alter responses and impulses due to an emotional experience. Mindfulness has been shown to positively impact this skill (Sünbül & Güneri, 2019). Emotion regulation is at the core of many different mental health difficulties, including attention deficit hyperactivity issues, anxiety, impulse control issues, traumatic stress, and depression.

Two separate systems manage emotional responses in the brain: the explicit, "top-down" system and the implicit, "bottom-up" system. Top-down emotion regulation utilizes executive functioning to consciously engage in strategies that reduce emotional distress. When you feel anxious about an upcoming exam or presentation and decide to distract yourself by focusing your attention elsewhere, you are making use of the top-down emotion regulation system. The top-down system requires active processing and internal thought to reduce emotional distress, and is housed largely in the prefrontal cortex (Guendelman, Medeiros, & Rampes, 2017). When emotions are generated through outside stimuli, the cognitive reappraisals that the top-down system utilizes are not very effective in regulating the emotional response. For example, if you notice a large spider next to your foot and become startled, trying to calm down by using a top-down strategy (e.g., reminding yourself that it is "just a spider") may not actually lessen your anxiety. Top-down regulation is much more helpful for emotions that originate from our conscious thought, because both the root of the emotion and the emotion regulation strategy occur through language. For example, if you think to yourself "My boss might fire me" after you show up to work late, you might begin feeling anxious. An effective top-down strategy might be to remind yourself of all the times you have arrived at work on time or other positive qualities you hold as an employee (McRae, Misra, Prasad, Pereira, & Gross, 2012).

The implicit, "bottom-up" regulation system is affect driven and occurs outside of conscious awareness. The bottom-up system utilizes the parts of the brain that monitor bodily arousal. When you experience stress, you might notice your heart racing, muscles tightening, or breath shortening. The bottom-up system in the body works through brain structures such as the anterior insula, anterior cingulate cortex, and dorsal medial prefrontal cortex to automatically regulate physical responses to stress and restore equilibrium (Guendelman et al., 2017). The bottom-up system may be more effective in lessening emotional reactions that are generated in a bottom-up fashion (McRae et al., 2012). If that same spider came back and startled you again, focusing on your breath may actually be a better strategy for calming down.

Because the top-down and bottom-up systems utilize different parts of the brain, neuroimaging studies have helped uncover which route mindfulness works through to improve emotion regulation. Mindfulness meditation can make use of both systems, but there is more evidence for the unique role of mindfulness in bolstering the bottom-up regulation system due to the way mindfulness promotes a connection to the body. Many mindfulness meditations begin by bringing attention to the breath, which promotes connection to the body systems that help regulate arousal. Monitoring and focusing on specific bodily sensations, such as the temperature of one's skin or the feeling of air filling up the lungs, is another way that mindfulness engages the bottom-up system and strengthens emotion regulation (Guendelman et al., 2017).

Mindfulness can bring extended emotion-regulation benefits for long-term meditators (see Figure 1.3). When shown photos that elicit negative emotion, long-term mindfulness meditators have less response in brain areas responsible for automatic emotional response. However, changes in the brain systems involved in emotion regulation can occur in the short term as well. Those who engaged in 8-week mindfulness meditation training programs

Figure 1.3. Mindfulness Can Help a Chaotic Mind Become More Organized.

Box 1.2 Mindfulness in Action

The positive changes in emotional regulation resulting from mindfulness practices should have implications for the way we think about rehabilitating and treating those with difficulties regulating their emotions and behavior. The Alternative to Incarceration Program in New York City—which allows participants to remain in the community while participating in mandatory programming instead of spending time in prison—utilizes mindfulness practices as a part of the rehabilitation process. After taking part in yoga and mindfulness training, males aged 18–24 participating in the program noted improvements in their ability to manage emotions and control impulses using mindfulness breathing techniques. One young man reported, "I can feel my pressure go up, it's like my mind is not thinking. It's like, once it goes up, it's clogging my mind. ... But then I start doing the breathing, it starts bringing my—I feel the pressure going down, my blood pressure going down, and I start thinking clearly" (Barrett, 2017, p. 1733).

showed strengthened connectivity between the amygdala and the ventral medial prefrontal cortex, areas of the brain involved in fear and risk processing (Kral et al., 2018).

Increased Compassion in Relationships

Compassion, care, and empathy for others begins, unintuitively enough, with compassion for ourselves. Self-compassion involves being kind and understanding to yourself in the face of failings and not increasing your own suffering by heaping on self-criticism. Self-compassion is associated with greater connection with others and with the recognition that being imperfect is a part of the human experience (Neff, 2011). Mindfulness interventions enhance self-compassion by increasing self-awareness, directing one's attention back to the present, and decentering from emotional experiences. Once you establish kindness and compassion toward yourself, you can extend the same compassion and empathy to others (Germer, 2014); you can see a broader spectrum of the "invisible" factors that influence other's choices and better understand their experience (Beaudoin, 2014). If you do not experience compassion for another's suffering, it is usually because the complexity of the other's experience is underestimated (Beaudoin, 2010). Longtime mindfulness meditators can develop this self-compassion through a decentered and broader view, and they demonstrate increased brain functioning in areas relating to empathy (Atkinson, 2013). This increase in self-compassion leads to an increase in positive mental states toward both themselves and others (Rodrígues-Carvajal, García-Rubio, Paniagua, García-Diex, & De Rivas, 2016).

Mindfulness practices and mindful traits, such as being present focused, aware of bodily sensations, and decentered from emotional reactions, also have benefits for relationships. Mindfulness helps increase attunement within relationships, meaning that you become more aware of others' body language and words, in the same way a musician is attuned to the notes of their instrument (Khaddouma, Gordon, & Bolden, 2015). Additionally, mindfulness can lead to better communication and higher satisfaction within relationships, and it increases how connected one feels to others (Barnes, Brown, Krusemark, Campbell, & Rogge, 2007).

Mindfulness practices can positively impact the sense of belonging and shared experience within a group as well. When a group engages in a shared experience, neuroimaging research shows that brain activity synchronizes across the individuals within the group (Nummenmaa et al., 2012). This is particularly true when there is a shared emotional experience. For example, a group of people listening to an emotional narrative demonstrated synchronized brain activity, particularly in the auditory cortices, prefrontal cortex, striatum, and amygdala. This suggests that synchronization occurs within networks involved in sound processing and speech comprehension, as well as emotion and self-referential processing (Nummenmaa et al., 2014).

Because mindfulness practices invite participants into a shared emotional state of calmness or joy, group mindfulness could lead to similar synchronization.

Brain activity synchronization can also occur when individuals are encouraged to adopt a similar psychological perspective during an activity. A research study investigating this phenomenon asked participants to watch a 10-minute film as either a detective attempting to uncover a criminal or an interior decorator tasked with redecorating the film set. Brain activity synchronization occurred within the two groups (i.e., those acting as detectives and those acting as interior decorators), but differed between the two groups (Lahnakoski et al., 2014). This suggests that encouraging individuals to view a situation with a similar mind-set can facilitate unique synchronization specific to that experience. In mindfulness meditation, individuals are invited to connect to the present moment and to engage with their experience with a nonjudgmental perspective. Given these findings, it is possible that the adoption of a similar perspective among a group of mindfulness meditators can facilitate a similar neural experience, and therefore promote feelings of group cohesiveness and belonging.

In addition to increasing social connectedness, mindfulness meditation practice can also enhance one's connection to the natural world by bringing awareness to the present moment and one's surroundings. Some mindfulness practices, such as the loving kindness meditation, also invite participants to wish happiness, health, and strength toward all living things, which seems to heighten one's connection to nature (Kabat-Zinn, 2004, 2005). After mindfulness meditation, practitioners report a heighted connection with nature as well as an increased belief in climate change (Wang, Geng, Schultz, & Zhou, 2019). The relationship between mindfulness and connectedness with nature is bidirectional—practicing meditation can strengthen one's connection with nature, and being in nature can enhance mindfulness traits. A study that required participants to spend 30 minutes in nature daily for 1 month showed significant increases in mindfulness traits, even in the absence of formal mindfulness training (Schutte & Malouff, 2018).

Benefits for Body Regulation

Mindfulness practices not only help us monitor the sensations of the body but also facilitate physiological changes in the body. The most stunning example of this lies with the Tibetan *g tummo* meditation practitioners. During *g tummo* practice, seasoned meditators can increase the temperature of their fingers and toes—the extremities that are the first to lose heat—by up to 8.3 degrees Celsius or 14.94 degrees Fahrenheit (Benson et al., 1982).

The Tibetan meditators use two mindfulness strategies in order to achieve this amazing change in body temperature: breathing and imagery. The Forceful Breath is an important part of this meditation, which increases body temperature by increasing arousal, the same way you might begin to feel warmer when engaging in physical activity. G *tummo* also includes imagery—the Tibetan meditators visually imagine themselves next to a source of heat, such as a flame, and conjure the sensation of warmth in their body. This imagery allows the meditators to heat their body past the normal cooling response point when our body typically begins to sweat (Kozhevnikova, Elliot, Shephard, & Gramann, 2013).

As the practice of the Tibetan meditators highlights, mental imagery can be a powerful tool. Research on motor learning shows that when we imagine doing a task, the motor cortex in our brain activates the same way it would if we were actually doing the task. Because of this, imagining the experience of specific tasks can lead to the same changes in the brain as physically practicing the tasks (Frank & Schack, 2017). While engaging in imagery does not necessarily strengthen muscles, it does strengthen the connection between the brain and the body. Using our imagination, we can trick our brains into thinking that we are engaging in the real deal, which is how the Tibetan meditators manage to raise their body temperature. Mindfulness meditation provides a space where our imagination can create a reality within our bodies, and Chapter 8 of this book provides an opportunity for participants to experiment with this idea using a self-warming experience.

Because of the implications for body regulation, mindfulness practices can be useful in preventive measures and the treatment of chronic diseases. There is evidence that mindfulness practices can improve autonomic nervous system functioning and blood pressure. Mindfulness traits, such as being present-focused and attuned to the body, are associated with the ability to maintain equilibrium in the autonomic nervous system as evidenced by measures of heart rate variability (HRV). HRV is a measure of the variation of time between each heartbeat. When you are in a time of continual stress, the variation is low because you are continually aroused. Mindfulness traits are associated with the ability to maintain a high HRV, which demonstrates high flexibility, adaptability, and resilience to different situations (Sun, Hu, Pan, Liu, & Huang, 2019). Mindfulness-based interventions are utilized as a part of treatment for a variety of medical illnesses, including diabetes and coronary heart disease. Mindfulness interventions have been shown to reduce blood pressure (Solano López, 2018) and can lead to improved sleep in those with diabetes or coronary heart disease. Mindfulness practices also promote more accepting approaches to illness (Keyworth et al., 2014).

Box 1.3 Mindfulness in Action

In addition to improving emotional regulation and influencing the functioning of the brain, mindfulness practices can also improve our immune system function. As you prepare for next winter's flu season, mindfulness practices may give you an extra boost. Researchers at the University of Wisconsin tested the effect of mindfulness on the immune system by providing an 8-week mindfulness meditation training program for randomly assigned employees at a biotechnology company. After completing the mindfulness program, the researchers gave the flu vaccination to both the participants and their coworkers who did not engage in the mindfulness training. The mindfulness meditators had a heightened immune system response to the vaccine, demonstrating increased amounts of antibodies responding to the influenza virus in the vaccine (Davidson et al., 2003).

It is possible that mindfulness meditation influences bodily regulatory systems partially because of the way this practice reduces stress and increases emotion regulation, both of which are related to physical health. For example, women undergoing in vitro fertilization (IVF) may experience continued difficulty becoming pregnant due to the emotional and physical burden of infertility treatment. A mindfulness intervention at a fertility medical center for women undergoing IVF combated the negative emotional experience by increasing self-compassion, adaptive emotional regulation, and positive coping, all of which led to significantly improved pregnancy rates (Li, Long, Liu, He, & Li, 2016).

Role of Mindfulness in Pain Management

Pain is more than just an automatic sensation in the body—the perception of pain is significantly impacted by the psychological and emotional experience of a sensation. Pain originates as a signal from the body to the brain, indicating that something is not right. However, this signal is processed by the emotional center of our brain, which can actually intensify the pain by attaching an emotional and evaluative experience to the sensation (Hansen & Streltzer, 2005). For example, after competitive athletes take a tough fall, they may get up and continue to play even though they are injured. They are preoccupied with the game and therefore may not react to pain from their injury. When walking home, those same athletes may still let out a yelp when they stub their toe because the context is different—all attention is now on the throbbing in their toe, and they may think about how much it hurts or about how careless they were. Mindfulness meditation lessens the perception of pain by targeting the psychological and emotional experience of the pain signal, which promotes increased pain acceptance, reduced pain catastrophizing, and reduced pain intensity (Day, Jensen, Ehde, & Thorn, 2014). This does not mean that meditators just "grin and bear" the pain or force their focus elsewhere—mindfulness interventions encourage meditators to be observers of their body and to notice the sensation of pain. However, instead of getting swept up in the resulting cascade of emotions and thoughts, mindfulness meditation encourages those in pain to notice the sensation in a nonjudgmental fashion and then to return their attention to the breath. Because of this present-focused attitude of acceptance, the posture and skills of mindfulness practices are often more effective at alleviating pain intensity and unpleasantness than just shifting attention (Zeidan et al., 2015).

Mindfulness practices are now a part of the recommended treatments for persons with chronic pain. Chronic pain is a condition of pain sensation that lasts for more than 3 months, and can in many cases last for the duration of one's life. While it may not be possible to completely eliminate pain in this condition, mindfulness interventions help those with chronic pain learn meditation practices that lead to increased functioning and well-being even

Box 1.4 Mindfulness in Action

Mindfulness practices can also be beneficial in acute pain experiences. For example, pregnant women who participated in mindfulness training during their third trimester were less afraid of the pain associated with birth and felt more prepared than pregnant women who took a childbirth education class. This mindfulness intervention, Mind in Labor, is taught at the University of California–San Francisco Medical Center. The program targets the anxiety many new parents have about giving birth by using mindfulness to give expecting parents tools to cope with pain and fear during labor. Mind in Labor participants practice enduring uncomfortable physical sensations and staying anchored in the present moment. This helps women manage the pain of contractions and remember that the pain will pass. In addition to feeling more prepared for birth, the women who participated in the mindfulness training utilized less medical intervention for pain during birth and had lower levels of depression during the postpartum period (Duncan et al., 2014).

in the midst of discomfort or disability. After receiving mindfulness training, those with chronic lower back pain, migraines, and musculoskeletal issues reported improvements in how much their pain bothered them and how much discomfort they perceived. Additionally, those with chronic pain who practiced mindfulness increased their overall health and functioning, and reported that pain did not interfere with their lives as much as it did before they began meditating (Majeed, Ali, & Sudak, 2018).

Attitude of Gratitude and Openness

Many mindfulness meditations center on the cultivation of gratitude (see Figure 1.4). Kabat-Zinn (2015), a mindfulness expert and pioneer in the integration of mindfulness into Western medicine and psychology, holds that gratitude for the present moment is one of the crucial attitudes of mindfulness practices. Mindfulness meditation helps us reflect on things that we often take for granted—that we are here, we are alive, our organs are working, and we are breathing. The attitude of gratitude in mindfulness reflects a quality of thankfulness and a readiness to act kindly or show appreciation to others (Kornfield, 1993). The cultivation of gratitude through mindfulness may be partially responsible for many of the previously discussed benefits of mindfulness. Gratitude acts as a mediator between mindfulness and beneficial

Figure 1.4. An Attitude of Gratitude, Openness, and Calmness Is at the Center of Mindfulness Practices.

outcomes, including self-acceptance and positive relations with others. Mindfulness-generated gratitude also increases one's feeling of self-efficacy and ability to navigate the world (Voci, Veneziani, & Fuochi, 2019).

The regular practice of gratitude has many benefits, including increased life satisfaction and having a clear purpose in life, even when controlling for other factors such as social support or individual resilience (Chen, Wu, & Chang, 2017). Gratitude practices, such as making a list of the things that inspire gratefulness or expressing gratitude toward another person, can even be helpful in decreasing symptoms of depression and improving overall psychological well-being (Harbaugh & Vasey, 2014). In addition to individual health benefits, gratitude can promote prosocial behavior and generosity. In a longitudinal study of middle school students, Froh, Bono, and Emmons (2010) found that gratefulness acted as a motivator for these students to engage with their community and help others.

Another attitude that Kabat-Zinn (2015) identifies as core to mindfulness is a nonjudgmental posture—in mindfulness meditation, we aim to be neutral observers of our environment and ourselves. Our judgments of things we like, do not like, and do not understand filter our perception of reality and may keep us from trying new things. Through a nonjudgmental view of the world, mindfulness can bolster openness to different experiences. The mindfulness practices of engaging in observation of the self and the surrounding world within the present moment encourage an expansion of our world view and allow us to be open to new perspectives (Spinhoven, Huijbers, Zheng, Ormel, & Speckens, 2017).

Summary

As this review of fascinating research highlights, the practice of mindfulness leads to innumerable benefits. It can improve cognition, keep our brains looking young and healthy, and reduce the experience of stress, even when outside circumstances do not change. Mindfulness practices also highlight the connection between the mind and body—we can influence our body regulation systems, including our body temperature, heart rate, blood pressure, and even the experience of pain! Finally, mindfulness meditation allows us to connect outside of ourselves with the natural world and other people in our lives. These benefits can be life changing for almost everyone, including those struggling with focus, emotion regulation, disconnection, chronic pain, and relational difficulties. How can we best help participants of all ages reap these formidable benefits? Let's move to Chapter 2, where we explore facilitation techniques that create a nonjudgmental and welcoming environment where everyone can practice mindfulness successfully.

CHAPTER TWO

Facilitating Engaging Experiences of Mindfulness

Intentions

Mindfulness meditation offers the possibility of developing a greater awareness of our mind, body, relationships, and surrounding environment. Another way to think of this practice is that it wakes up, activates, and illuminates a biological human ability that few people know they have. Brain research has confirmed that mindfulness meditation ignites a separate and specialized part of the brain that isn't active during day-to-day autopilot life, unless one makes a concerted effort to be mindful (Farb et al., 2007). The human brain's ability to be mindful is a well-hidden inner treasure, and facilitating this experience has to be done thoughtfully.

The exercises featured in this book have been successful for participants of all ages. Once mindful awareness is activated, people have access to significantly more information and are surprised by what they discover. They often want to share and ponder on the experience, and sometimes need help to make sense of it all. A common result of these discoveries is also that people can entertain and choose from a much greater number of responses and options when faced with an internal or external challenge. They can choose what they really want to focus on right now, whether they'd like to intensify or reduce their body's physiological activation, if they want to engage with a negative emotion, if a relational interaction is going in a constructive direction or should be redirected, or how they can actively modify their experience of pain and suffering.

The journey into becoming mindful can be divided into four levels:

1. Tasting: a developing awareness of oneself and what is possible to experience;
2. Seeking: an increasing frequency of moments when mindful awareness is intentionally engaged and an ability to mitigate some reactions;
3. Cultivating: more consistent efforts to be mindfully focused and emotionally calm in daily life, even in the face of unexpected events;
4. Living: embodying a mindful lifestyle where the ability to be in a peaceful state and respond calmly to any situation is acquired and sustained through daily practice.

Some could argue that additional stages of mindfulness are attained by Buddhist monks or by revered leaders such as the Dalai Lama or Thich Nhat Hanh, whose diligent 4–5 hours per day of practice leads to indescribable states. The realization of these different steps depends mostly on individuals' commitment to practice outside of the teaching context, and on the quality of their practice. It may also fluctuate throughout a lifetime, with more diligent, extensive mindfulness practice during one period of life (like before having children!), and more sporadic practice when lives become overly saturated with electronics, stress, or busyness.

Some participants may not currently go beyond the "tasting" stage, while others will want to immerse themselves in the rigorous practice of these skills. This is a personal and logistical decision. Mentioning these different levels can help participants have more realistic expectations and make a conscious decision about the journey they wish to undertake. The programs outlined in this book allow people to explore these four levels, although people wanting to attain Level 4 would definitely need to practice on a daily basis, whether on their own, through an app, or by listening to recordings of the exercises.

The exercises included in this book were initially created for group settings, which offer several advantages:

- Greater commitment to practicing because of the group's common goal;
- Learning from one another's struggles;
- Sense of community and belonging growing throughout the shared journey;
- Richer discussions with more observations from varied perspectives.

While groups provide the ideal setting, we are also aware that this is not always possible. Most of the exercises have also been facilitated in individual therapy, coaching, or consultation settings, especially those from the breathing, nature meditations, and Lords of the Rings chapters. When these exercises are practiced in individual settings, facilitators can slightly adjust and tailor them for each individual.

General Facilitation Considerations

Facilitating a mindfulness meditation experience is both similar and different to other group processes. It is similar in that participants can gain benefits from a charismatic, committed, engaging, and safe facilitator whom people enjoy listening to. It is different from other psycho-educational contexts in that facilitators must truly model a calm, present-focused state of mind that participants may have seldom experienced or witnessed in their lives. While instructors with various levels of experience can use the exercises taught in this book, it is ideal if the facilitator can enter the coveted state of mindful presence during the facilitation. We discuss this more in what follows, along with tips for engaging the audience, common issues, and how to avoid preventable problems.

Mindful Presence

The facilitator's mindful presence will set the tone for the exercise and allow participants to have a model. The state of mindful presence involves being present focused, accepting what is, and connecting with one's body (Brandsma, 2017). These manifest for the facilitator as an unconditionally kind attitude, a stance of openness, and embodiment.

Unconditionally Kind Mind-Set

Mindfulness is about withholding judgment and observing what is without reacting. It is important for facilitators to treat each participant with this attitude as well—this will create an open, welcoming space where participants are invited to engage in what may feel like a vulnerable activity to some, depending on the space and the context. Give heartfelt attention to each participant, if possible. One way to demonstrate kindness is through a "yes, and" mind-set (Beaudoin & Walden, 1998), where any comment participants make is acknowledged and received in a positive, validating way (the "yes"), with the facilitator adding relevant and enriching ideas afterward (the "and"). For example, if a participant stated, "I felt very calm; it was wonderful, but at some point I became distracted as it reminded me of when I went to my grandparent's home in the countryside which I loved so much"; a facilitator could reply as follows: "It's wonderful that you felt so calm (the *yes*); the metaphor reminded you of special moments in your life, *and* this is often because our memory works by emotional associations—when we're in a certain emotional state, our mind will remind us automatically of other times in our life we were in that state! You can try to acknowledge the memory and gently bring your mind back to the present time."

Openness

An attitude of openness and flexibility is paramount in mindfulness practices. As the facilitator, it is important to embody an attitude of openness to new ideas or unexpected events, as it will set the mood for the mindfulness exercise. If you are open to hearing about and making space for others, they will be more likely to share their experiences. This is important, as the discussion portion of the exercises is as valuable as the mindfulness meditation itself. Participants will uncover a great variety of sensations and observations, some of which they may appreciate, and others that will trouble them. There is more than one way to experience awareness, and all of them are valid.

Embodiment

Embodiment, or the connection to sensations within the body, has become a fascinating scientific field in the past decade. Embodiment provides a body-based grounding for thoughts, feelings, and behaviors. More specifically, in the past, we knew that when we are happy, we smile; we now know that when we smile, our brains can more easily enter a state of happiness (Beaudoin & Duvall, 2017). A number of exercises highlighted in this book encourage participants to take notice of the body sensations associated with their focused and relaxed state, so that they can more readily cultivate and replicate this state. Ideally, facilitators have experimented with the exercises before facilitating them and can therefore comment on embodied observations, making it easier for participants to notice their own. It is important to try the exercises before facilitating them, and observe, for example, how *you* feel when your arm is stretched or when you breathe rapidly. Practicing ahead of time can help facilitators generate words to describe the novel bodily experiences of their participants. Because people often pay more attention to their mind than their body, they may be out of practice in naming bodily sensations, which makes the labeling of these sensations by facilitators very helpful. The Fascinating Body Parts chapter is the epitome of increasing embodied awareness.

Importance of a Facilitator Role Model

Participants will get an inner experience of the facilitator's meditative state through mirror neurons, which are special cells in our brain that help facilitate social interaction and empathy. When we see another person taking an action, the mirror neurons in our brain fire in the same way as if we were taking that action, allowing us to embody the experience of the other person (Iacoboni, 2009). For example, if you see someone smiling, your mirror neurons for smiling will fire as well. In a group setting, if participants see the facilitator adopting a posture of mindfulness, the mirror neuron system will allow them to more easily come into that experience.

Participants will also feel others around them get into a deep state, and their mirror neurons will pick that up, making it slightly easier for everyone to do the same. As discussed in Chapter 1, synchronicity research shows that each person in a group can contribute a little push into a deeper shared state, which can have a snowball effect, allowing beginners to attain states they may not have been able to attain on their own.

Engaging Your Group

In the present-focused spirit of mindfulness, facilitators can become fully attentive to their own and participants' experiences, and this is *more important* than sticking to a script. The transcripts provided are only examples. Facilitators are encouraged to make them their own, to use language that fits the subculture of their audience, and to add stories or examples about their own life adventures when relevant. Please do *not* simply *read* an entire transcript to your audience! It would be difficult for participants to connect with you and the material. The result would likely be a bored and disconnected audience! Ideally, facilitators speak of this material with passion, fascination, and enthusiasm, which will make the material very appealing. The following suggestions are just a few ways to imbue this passion and enthusiasm into your group and to help your participants continuously build on their skills.

Leading with Conviction

Leadership in mindfulness meditation involves being ready to immerse oneself fully in a practice without fear of others' judgments. Three of the exercises featured in this book involve making a sound (i.e., Ocean Harmony, Humming Colony, and Laughing Rhythms). The facilitator will need to initiate the sounds and set the tone with loud conviction and feelings of safety. This is not the time to be shy, as it would indicate that even you, as a facilitator, do not feel safe! This has to be like jumping in cold water; if you decide to facilitate this exercise, take a deep breath and vocalize. Additionally, we also encourage you to lead with humility. Even if you have more experience than your audience, they can still help you progress in your own journey as well.

Silence and Stillness

It can be incredibly difficult to quiet one's mind during meditation if the surrounding space is loud and agitated, particularly for beginning meditators. It is important to attempt to create a relatively quiet, calm space before beginning a meditation exercise. If you hear a participant making noise that may be distracting to others, you can gently redirect the entire group without singling out that individual by saying something like, "*Let's all check in with our breath, and make sure we are breathing in and out through the nose, keeping the mouth closed.*" If a person is talking or wiggling, say, "*Try to see if you can make your body still and not move a single muscle so we can all enjoy the silence.*"

Absolute silence can be intimidating for some people—we live in a busy world with nearly constant noise and movement coming from cars, music, televisions, or other people in the background. It is important that facilitators feel comfortable in silence, as the group will likely reflect facilitators' comfort levels. Try to balance offering clear directives (which reduces the likelihood of minds wandering) with silent moments for the group to attain a mindful presence of their own. When figuring out if you should talk during silence, as the facilitator, go by the old adage: "Speak only if it improves upon the silence."

Continuity

As with all developing skills, the journey into mindfulness requires scaffolding from one week to the next. It is ideal to start each session with examples of how participants applied the ideas from the previous week in their lives. Questions such as the following are typically evocative: "Who thought of the ideas we discussed last week, after the session?" "Did anyone do anything slightly different this week in light of last session's material?" In general, taking the feedback of three or four people may inspire others who may not have applied the material in their day-to-day lives yet, and enrich everyone's sense of possible applications. This process keeps the ideas alive from week to week.

Common Participant Issues

Participants' Chattering

Participants' chattering at inappropriate times needs consideration. If it is only occasional, a visual encouragement or nonverbal reminder to stay silent can usually be effective. If it is frequent or disruptive enough to interfere with the experience of others, the facilitator can kindly ask that people pay attention and not talk over one another, so the group can hear everyone's contributions and participants can immerse themselves in the exercises without distractions. If needed, facilitators can organize brief group discussions before the exercises with questions such as "what kind of context is most conducive for learning and practicing, for each one of you?" Facilitators may choose to highlight visual images, silences, questions, lack of interruption, confidentiality, etc. in addition to participants' suggestions. If the situation is seriously interfering, then an individual conversation with the offending participant may be warranted.

Wandering Minds

Jack Kornfield (1993) often says: "The mind is like a puppy; you tell it to stay, it will stay for a couple of minutes then wander off again" (see Figure 2.1). During the mindfulness exercises, it is likely that participants will have this experience. It is important to actively remind people that their minds *will* wander, and it is part of the exercise. As the facilitator, you can kindly remind them to bring their focus back to the present exercise. It is crucial to name this for participants in order to prevent feelings of failure and temptation to give up when they find their minds wandering. Various exercises presented in this book use imagination to engage the attention system. However, imagination can also encourage minds to wander. Imagination is most useful for creating an intriguing context and for fostering access to inner experiences

Figure 2.1. The Mind Is Like a Puppy; You Tell It to Stay, It Will Stay for a Few Minutes Then Wander Off Again.

people may have never attained before in their lives. At other times, the focus should be on awareness and on simply being present to whatever arises. Facilitators should plan on reminding people regularly to bring their minds back to the present task, even if it is not in the script: "When your mind wanders away, gently bring it back to the present moment."

Participants Over-Participating

If participants are over-participating in a way that is taking away from the group experience, the facilitator can acknowledge that they would like to give a speaking opportunity to as many people as possible, or if necessary, go around the circle so everyone has a turn to share. The latter is least preferred, however, as it puts pressure on people to talk, which can create anxiety and reduce the beneficial effects of the experience.

Participants Under-Participating

When a participant remains mostly silent in the discussions over and over again, facilitators may wish to ask for written reflections on people's experiences to better understand if there is an issue. This can occur because of shyness or a reluctance to extract oneself from a deep relaxed state. It is also sometimes because of feeling unsafe to talk (in a classroom, for example) or feeling unable to attain the focused states everyone else is discussing, and feeling marginalized as a result. If the last two concerns are present, a brief conversation after the session may be helpful.

Physical Posture

A straight posture is more conducive to mindfulness meditation. Notice how people are holding their bodies and insert additional instructions if you see someone slouched. For example: "*On the next in-breath, imagine your head and shoulder being lifted by a string toward the sky, as if you were a puppet being straightened into perfect alignment.*" This is particularly important throughout the breathing exercise chapter, where many of the practices would simply be ineffective for a slouched person who is completely compressing their diaphragm (Stahl & Goldstein, 2010). For participants for whom this is challenging, attempt to facilitate exercises while standing or lying down.

Congestion, Itching, and Physical Discomfort

Common issues that invariably arise with a group include a participant whose nose is clogged or who feels physically uncomfortable. For nose congestion, participants can focus on the air actually passing through their nose (*not* the restricted sensation), even if it's a sliver of air, and the mental focus

Figure 2.2. The Itch Problem.

and relaxed state in itself can sometimes help open up the airways. Otherwise, they can partly breathe through their mouth. If it is an issue of pain, they can preemptively plan a position that will minimize risk of worsening their condition such as lying down or sitting on a chair of specific height. Beyond that, it is an exercise of delinking sensations of pain from their emotional reactions and the tendency to add tension to those areas of the body. Participants have to learn to observe discomfort in a detached way, noticing its shape, density, color, and temperature, just as you would observe a blotch of cream on your skin. Chapters 4 and 5 offer wonderful strategies for dealing with pain. Having an itch provides an incredible opportunity to practice letting go, observing, and not engaging with it emotionally. It is a gift, as we know it is inconsequential and allows experimenting with the mind as illustrated in Figure 2.2.

Safety and Health

Mindfulness meditation is considered extremely safe for people of all ages, and has even been found to improve a number of medical conditions, as discussed in Chapter 1. However, facilitators should recommend that participants who have medical conditions check with their doctors before engaging in the breathing exercises, as they have very real physiological effects. Those effects are usually beneficial, but it is advisable for participants struggling with seizures, asthma, hernias, or wearing a pacemaker, for example, to seek medical advice before attempting the exercises. Facilitators can also reassure their audience by mentioning that sometimes people might feel slightly dizzy or a little different after an exercise because they are not used to oxygenating their brains in this way. Slight dizziness is usually not a sign of any significant problem, and it tends to pass after a few minutes, leaving participants with a wonderful feeling of relaxation and clarity.

Avoiding Preventable Facilitation Problems

Mindlessness and Stress

In mindfulness practices, the only time that matters is NOW. In fact, the only time when we ever have power is now. Facilitators, however, just as everyone else, can experience days that are more stressful than others. Ideally, facilitators can block these personal issues and focus on the present meditation without allowing them to alter the session. If you are a novice of mindfulness, or if the concern is particularly hard to block, it is often better to acknowledge it and be honest. You can all be on a team together, each trying to cultivate a better version of yourself.

Unrealistic Expectations

Explain what is possible to attain with practice, and acknowledge that each person will attain what their life experience and body allows them to reach at this time. Everyone has a different starting place, will learn more from some formats rather than others, and will come across different challenges, and therefore everyone will end at a slightly different place. This learning is also not linear. Some people may struggle at the very beginning for several weeks, and then suddenly make a leap in progress. Others have a steady journey of improvement. What matters most is to keep going and not become discouraged.

Homework and Practice

In order to develop a deepening sense of mindfulness, participants are encouraged to practice the week's material at home. No magic is involved; it is all about practicing the "muscles" that control the mind, and thinking differently about the ups and downs of life. The original and wonderful mindfulness stress reduction program of Jon Kabat-Zinn assigns weekly readings to discuss at each meeting. If you are facilitating this process with a committed group of participants, and would like to enrich the training with such additions, it is highly recommended to add readings. Many books on the subject are worth perusing, and reading a chapter every night will help participants remain anchored in these ideas on a daily basis. You may wish to even add 30 minutes to your session for people to discuss the readings.

Length, Pace, and Other Notions of Time

Busy and distracted people are in the habit of moving fast and being hurried—everything is ruled by the clock. In some settings, it may be valuable to ask participants to remove their watch and place it safely with their other belongings, in order to practice being without the clock ticking. This can facilitate the experience of simply being in the present time, feeling each second of life go by, and looking inward. You can remind adult participants that from a mindfulness perspective, we try to dwell "in the now and pay brief visits to past and future when required" (Tolle, 2004), i.e. after the session!

Historically, mindfulness is practiced for shorter periods of time at first (such as with the breathing exercises) and is progressively increased to longer periods of concentration (such as the Lords of the Rings exercises). It is also best to end when everyone is feeling some success and still enjoying themselves rather than to drag a practice on for too long. The times listed for each exercise are only estimates and may or may not fit perfectly with your group size, population, or mood of the day. If an exercise ends much too early for the window of time allocated in the session, it is always possible to ask people to draw, describe, or write about the moment when they experienced themselves in the most satisfying way during the practice.

Considerations When Facilitating with Young People

When facilitating the mindfulness exercises presented in this book, it is important to consider your audience from a developmental perspective. The factors that contribute to success and sustained attention look different for various age groups—for example, adults tend to like more concrete facts, teens may like information that relates to identity and relationships, and children tend to enjoy imagination. Through our experience of facilitating these exercises with children and adolescents, we have a few additional tips for working with youth.

Frame the Experience

Giving youth a solid and concrete outline of the exercise and what the expectations are can help them remain focused on the task at hand. Before beginning a mindfulness exercise, it is helpful to remind and explain that in order to engage in mindfulness, it is important to have a quiet atmosphere, which means waiting to chat with your friend until afterward. It is also good to explain to the group ahead of time that you as the facilitator will be asking questions during the mindfulness exercise, but these questions are just for the participants to think about and not to answer aloud. Asking questions during the setup can be a good way to engage students with the instructions and to ensure that the youth understand what you are explaining. For example, you might say, "*Let's check if everyone heard that: Will you talk if I ask you a question during the exercise? [NO!]*"

Make the Exercise Relevant

Youth are more likely to be enthusiastic and engaged if the material feels relevant to their lives. As the facilitator, you can add questions relevant to their day to keep young minds engaged. For example, the facilitator might ask: "*Who can give me an example of a moment when you were mindful on the field trip yesterday?*" Such questions can be inserted in three different segments of the presentations:

1. During the introduction in order to set up the intrigue;
2. When engaging young people to connect with their life or reflect on their experience;
3. During the discussion following the mindfulness exercise.

Consider the Context

Depending on the environment or setting in which you facilitate, there may be a need for a partner or an assistant. This is especially relevant in school settings, when groups may be facilitated within students' classrooms. In this case, it is crucial to collaborate with teachers on what the expectations are, where you would like students to sit, and how you will handle students not participating or struggling to sustain attention. It is important to be on the same page as teachers beforehand—this will help you prevent being stuck in avoidable binds. For example, if you do not discuss how you will handle children becoming distracted (which will happen!), a teacher may react in a punitive or strict way in an effort to be helpful, which may actually cause the children to shut down and not engage. Teachers can be wonderful allies during the exercises, particularly if they can help redirect children and keep them on task in a friendly, positive way, such as sitting beside a child. Additionally, many teachers find the mindfulness exercises personally helpful, and they can be encouraged to participate in the exercise and discussion if they would like.

Have an Exit Strategy

When facilitating exercises with youth, it is important to not make promises you cannot keep. You want to balance sharing a plan at the onset, with ensuring the exercise will end on a positive note. Because of this, it can be helpful to keep the outline vague in order to allow for flexibility in the exercise, just in case youth are distracted that particular day or something is not clicking for them. For example, if you were going to facilitate a partnered exercise, instead of telling the group that they are going to do three rounds with different partners, you might want to say that they will be working with partners (and avoid mentioning three). This will avoid feelings of disappointment and guilt in the case that children become too distracted and you have to end early. Before beginning the exercise, think about a way to gracefully end the exercise early if needed in order to ensure that the group ends on a positive and mindful note.

Summary

Our role as facilitators is to open intriguing paths and to mirror the intricate value in each person's unique journey. As such, it is important to create a space that feels safe for concentrating and taking risks. This can be accomplished by following the tips in this chapter, and by offering an unwavering confidence in each participant's ability to move forward in their mindfulness journey. The following chapter outlines captivating ways of engaging busy, distracted minds in an individual or group setting: by recruiting the brain's attention systems!

CHAPTER THREE

Recruiting the Brain's Attention Systems to Better Facilitate a Successful Experience of Mindfulness

People talk at a rate of 125–180 words per minute, and the brain is able to process 400–600 words per minute. So while someone is talking, you can, at the same time, make a list of things to do and plan dinner. While you will probably not contribute many creative, supportive, or profound thoughts to the speaker's life, you might still be able to repeat exactly what they told you when accused of not listening!

This ability to process many streams of thought at the same time backfires when focused attention or quality listening is required, whether in relationships,

Figure 3.1. While These Office Workers May Absorb Some of What Everyone Is Saying, They May Not Have a Very Productive or Interesting Meeting without Stopping to Listen!

Figure 3.2. Sometimes Multitasking Doesn't Quite Turn Out the Way We Thought It Would.

parenting, education, or mindfulness training (see Figure 3.1). Unfortunately, as mentioned before, modern life has become saturated with stress, deadlines, overscheduling, and overstimulation of many kinds, leaving people more vulnerable than ever to developing the habit of mentally multitasking (see Figure 3.2), and not participating in any of those tasks very well (Ralph, Thomson, Cheyne, & Smilek, 2014). Minds that are constantly aroused by mental churning grow accustomed to this pace and become increasingly vulnerable to boredom and distractibility in the absence of intense stimulation. For example, office workers have been found to check their emails every 30 minutes (Kushlev & Dunn, 2015), and children now do their homework while listening to music, surfing the Internet, and receiving a regular flow of texts!

As a result, the gentle and slow-paced instructions in traditional mindfulness meditations may not capture minds accustomed to overstimulation, distraction, and busyness—these participants may mentally drift away within a few minutes of beginning an exercise. What do we know about the brain's attention systems that could help facilitators hook their participants' attention and better help them practice the crucial skills of meditating and focusing?

Box 3.1 Attention in Action

Researchers at the University of British Columbia set out to test the impact of less multitasking and email-checking among office workers, and limited office workers to checking their email just three times per day. Those who engaged in limited email use experienced significantly lower daily stress and reported feeling more positive emotions and social connectedness than those who could check their email as often as they wished (Kushlev & Dunn, 2015).

The Brain's Attention Systems

Attention comprises a series of complex processes that allow people to direct their focus to different sensations, information, or objects. At any given moment, the surrounding environment continually provides more input than the brain can fully process. Attention mechanisms help the brain be selective as to what kind of perceptual information makes it into conscious awareness. Few people realize that there are actually different attention networks in the brain: external, internal, and the lesser-known experiential system. External attentional control is focused on something in the environment, such as the wail of a siren, a cool breeze, or a sudden flash of light. It is based on sensory perception, as well as information about time and space. Internal attentional control is focused toward information that is already represented in the mind, such as a thought about a project at work or family members (Chun, Golomb, & Turk-Browne, 2011).

When the mind is in its "default" state, it tends to focus more on internal experiences with a steady stream of thoughts. The mind wanders, attending less to the present experience and focusing instead on plans for the weekend or whether anyone noticed your new haircut. However, there is another network in the brain known as the experiential network that is focused more on present experiences, directing attention to sensory experiences in a more objective manner. When using the experiential network, regions of the brain having to do with emotional responses and decision making (i.e., the ventral medial prefrontal cortex and the amygdala) are less active. This indicates that when utilizing the experiential network, the brain is able to attend to information in the present moment without passing a value judgment or attaching it to an emotional response. In the default network, nearly all thoughts have an attached value or emotion. The default network and the experiential network are inversely correlated—when one is completely active, the other is essentially inactive. Evidence suggests that the continued practice of mindfulness allows one to utilize the experiential network more frequently and effectively (Farb et al., 2007).

Because attention encompasses a wide variety of functions, mechanisms, and information, attention is a whole-brain process. Information can come through vision, touch, smell, hearing, taste, vestibular senses, and one's memory. The integration of the different modalities requires the involvement of many different brain areas, including the frontal and parietal cortices, specific sensory cortices, and subcortical structures such as the thalamus, basal ganglia, and cerebellum (Rosenberg et al., 2016).

Development of Attention Processes

The ability to direct and sustain attention over time develops with age. These processes begin to emerge soon after birth—babies can start to orient and attend to preferred over non-preferred objects as early as 3 months old (Plude, Enns, & Brodeur, 1994). As children grow older, they are able not only to orient to specific objects but also to ignore competing stimuli. This ability is referred to as inhibitory control and it increases the length of sustained attention (Reck & Hund, 2011). When children are 6 years old, this ability is still developing. Children at this age are learning how to ignore irrelevant stimuli, but they cannot do so for very long—sooner or later, they exhaust their ability to keep distractions out and become preoccupied with other stimuli. By age 12, children are able to ignore distractions for a significantly longer period of time (Zupan, Blagrove, & Watson, 2018).

Recruiting and Optimizing the Brain's Attention during Mindfulness Exercises

Our brain weighs about 10 pounds and comprises 2–3% of our body mass, but it uses about 20% of our energy. It is designed to conserve energy and focus only on material deemed worthy of attention. How can we make our mindfulness teachings worthy of the brain's attention when it has an immense daily reservoir of distracting experiences to process and reflect upon? In what follows, we list a few experiential attention boosters that will increase your chances of success, particularly with beginners. With continued mindfulness practice over time, the effort it takes to sustain attention decreases—experienced meditators show less frontal lobe activities during periods of meditation, suggesting that their attention does not require as much executive control to inhibit other stimuli or regulate attention (Tanaka et al., 2015).

What People Rarely Forget

Curiosity, the active desire to learn or know something, can fortify learning, shape the way one experiences the world, and enhance the likelihood of remembering new material. Curiosity may arise when there is a gap between what a person knows and what they would like to know, when something piques their interest, is novel, or seems like a stimulating challenge. When a person feels curious and is learning something new, the dopaminergic reward system within the brain is activated (Gottlieb, Oudeyer, Lopes, & Baranes, 2013). Since this experience is gratifying, people tend to focus their attention on what makes them curious. This means that if a mindfulness exercise can be intriguing, participants are more likely to listen to the directions than daydream and therefore are more likely to succeed in accessing satisfying deep meditative states. In addition, being highly curious is linked with non-defensiveness and nonjudgmental attitudes (Kashdan, Afram, Brown, Birnbeck, & Drvoshanov, 2011), which in itself can enhance the compassionate, objective stance in mindfulness and increase the likelihood of perceiving other experiences as neutral and positive rather than negative. Curiosity is easy to integrate in mindfulness teachings, and in fact, some would argue that it is essentially what mindfulness is about: being curious about the present moment. For example, the simple act of sharing fascinating facts about body parts before an exercise or asking participants intriguing questions during the facilitation process tends to pique their interest and curiosity.

How Intense Should It Be?

Attention processes are impacted by both high and low arousal states. When the body has a very high level of arousal, such as a flight/fight/freeze response to danger, the brain becomes hypervigilant and engages in a purposeful and effortful level of attention. Similar neurotransmitters activate bodily arousal and attentional alertness, including norepinephrine, orexin, and adenosine (Geiger, Neufang, Stein, & Domschke, 2014). However, the information that the brain attends to in these situations is generally limited to specific danger cues or risks of incurring pain. Attention can be enhanced through low arousal states as well, such as some forms of relaxation and mindfulness states (Bruya & Tang, 2018).

Concretely, how can we arouse the brain in a helpful manner during mindfulness training? We can do so by giving people a challenge and encouraging them to complete a task that seems difficult but within reach. In other words, a task within the zone of proximal development (Vygotsky, 1978) that may not be achievable by the person on their own, but has a great likelihood of success with support and guidance.

Box 3.2 Attention in Action

A Yoga Master in Japan claimed to not feel pain while he meditated. Understandably, researchers wanted to put this to the test! The Yoga Master underwent brain imaging after receiving noxious laser stimulation in order to see how he was handling the pain on a neurological level. The Yoga Master showed little to no brain activity in the areas of the brain typically associated with pain—instead, his brain activity looked similar to a person experiencing relaxation. This is an amazing example of the impact that dedicated, long-term mindfulness practice can have on our brain's interpretation of pain (Kakigi et al., 2005).

Involving Pain

Pain is a specific form of arousal that definitely gets people's attention! As mentioned earlier, the same brain regions tend to activate during physical *or* emotional pain, which means that physical and emotional regulation are intimately connected (Kabat Zinn, 1990, 2005). Consequently, practicing your ability to respond to physical pain will also help your ability to respond to emotional struggles, and vice versa (Salomons, Nusslock, Detloff, Johnstone, & Davidson, 2015). Announcing that pain will be an optional part of meditation training always perks participants' ears. Some research suggests that people are more likely to pay attention to a stimulus to avoid pain rather than to gain pleasure. Famous French philosopher Albert Camus has even stated that given how much humans grow when they are miserable, it can be said that happiness is a waste of time! While avoiding pain and seeking happiness may seem overlapping, they are not necessarily the same. All of the exercises in this book end with tests that involve some discomfort. Some of these tests are simply annoying sounds; others involve touching something unpleasant. None of the tasks are dangerous or overly painful, just an exciting opportunity for participants to test their skills. Knowing that mysterious tests are scheduled at the end of the program tends to motivate people, in a fun way, to pay attention to all of the skills and experiential practices facilitated. Such a short-term goal gives an immediate and concrete purpose to the training that can be more motivating than the general idea of bettering their lives.

Fluffy, Red, and Dazzling Elements!

As you can tell from reading this subtitle, visual information, metaphors, and imagery heighten people's attention! The optic nerve goes directly to the back of the head and relays visual information very quickly to the reptilian brain, our primitive, survival-focused center. Sight is the sense that receives by far the most attention in the brain—more than 80% of the information that enters the brain is visual (Jensen, 2008), and more than 50% of the cortex—the outer layer of the brain where higher thinking occurs—is devoted to visual information processing (Hagen, 2012). We all know that an image is worth a thousand words, so showing images at the beginning of a mindfulness session can increase the amount of relevant information that will be readily available to the mind during the exercise. This is particularly the case with many groups of people who do not pay as close attention to their visual surroundings because of their overly busy lifestyle or a high amount of stress (Sänger, Bechtold, Schoofs, Blaszkewicz, & Wascher, 2014).

ME-ning

Since people ascribe *meaning* to experiences that are most relevant to their own personal lives, the word could be playfully re-written as Me-ning! We tend to pay more attention to concepts, ideas, or experiences that are directly valuable to us, so the art of teaching and capturing attention involves helping people recognize that an information is personally impactful (Anderson, 2013). In fact, the *meaning* a person makes of what they see and hear is more predictive of levels of attention than an objective assesment of what they are seeing or hearing (Peacock, Hayes, & Henderson, 2019). The exercises in this book create a context for meaning-making *before* the exercise with intriguing information and discussion, and *after* the exercise with relevant questions, sharing, and observations. Most people will also better remember and revisit experiences that are meaningful, leading participants to want to practice the exercises at home and discuss them with their families.

Fire and Ice

Most people have been captured at some point or another by an image that skillfully contrasts two opposing scenes. Each concept alone may not have attracted any attention whatsoever, but the juxtaposition of the two opposite ideas highlights the disparities very clearly (see Figure 3.3).

Contrasts offer a couple of advantages: they intrigue people and they help the mind more easily notice phenomena that would otherwise escape their attention. This catchy technique can be very useful in teaching mindfulness. A common example of this practice is meditating on one foot and then asking participants to contrast the sensations between the foot we focused on, versus the one left unattended. While a participant may have felt that the foot was generally more relaxed, the comparison suddenly heightens the extent to which it feels different, and makes visible other aspects such as

Figure 3.3. Contrast Is a Powerful Attention-Grabber.

warmth, tingling, and density that may never have been noticed otherwise. These differences are generally very interesting to examine, and increase participants' awareness of the powerful impact of mindfulness on their bodies. Contrast can be used in many different ways, from visual images, to sensations in the body, to concepts, to various emotions arising at different stages of the mindfulness experience.

From Allocution to Talking

The use of accessible and culturally relevant language rather than complex vocabulary can go a long way in keeping participants engaged. Research shows that people are increasingly struggling with listening. Compared to previous generations, children and adults seem to be losing the ability of actively listening and retaining information that was shared even just a few minutes prior (Sullivan & Thompson, 2013).

The language used by the facilitator will have a significant impact on all participants' mental engagement in the exercises, and especially with children and adolescents, or different socioeconomic groups. This book offers transcripts for all the exercises, but the facilitator is urged to review, edit, and transform the instructions into a friendly text that will use the local vocabulary and be evocative to participants. In case of doubt, don't hesitate to substitute a transcript word for another that will be more likely to be understood. The general consensus is that when children are learning to read, they should encounter no more than three or four unknown words per page if a teacher wants them to persevere in reading a book. This rule of thumb can also apply here. The point of communicating is to be heard, so there is no use in risking a participant misunderstanding or being lost in the instructions when facilitating something already as challenging as meditating.

Tone of voice also matters. At the onset, facilitators benefit from being enthusiastic and engaging (Beaudoin & Walden, 1998). The goal of the introduction in each exercise is to help participants let go of their worries and the preceding events of the day, to engage in the here and now of the mindfulness experience. Another way to think of this is that you are competing for the mind's attention against what is already churning in a person's head. Once you have participants' attention, the mindfulness exercise itself will require a progressive slowing down of the tone of voice, with variations such as sometimes pausing, sometimes talking a little louder, and sometimes whispering. Varying the tone of voice slightly will contribute to sustaining attention.

The Crucial Instruction in the Middle

Participants will typically focus well at the beginning of the exercise and at the end. Research studying free recall shows that we attend to, and remember, items at the beginning and the end of a list much better than the items in the middle (Howard & Kahana, 1999). It is in the middle of the exercise that facilitators need to make efforts to keep busy minds engaged. Several ways of addressing these issues are included in this book. For example, the facilitator can announce ahead of time that there will be important instructions in the middle, such as when to slowly stand up. No one wants to be singled out and remain seated, so people usually make an extra effort to attend to the instructions. Another example is to remain interactive and use communications such as "raise a finger when you feel this."

Yes! versus NO!

Emotions are activated by certain words or tones of voice that remind us of our childhood or other experiences, ideas, and discussions. Emotions tend to activate the limbic system and engage the internal attention systems. In his book *Thinking Fast and Slow*, Kahneman (2011) explores people's focus during decision-making processes and concludes that contrary to intuition, it is not our most advanced cerebral region (the neocortex) that runs the show, but rather a combination of the more primitive areas: the reptilian (survival) and emotional brain. These two areas of the brain have a great impact on where people direct their attention and how they attend to information. Through stories and personal interviews, some of our exercises intentionally trigger emotions while inviting participants to remain calm observers of the situation, or even navigate from one emotion to the next. Emotions play the dual role of keeping people's attention on and actively developing regulation methods *during* the session.

"A Smile Is a Curve That Sets Everything Straight"

This wonderful quote by Phyllis Diller reminds us of the importance of smiles, laughter, and humor in any human interaction. Humor in particular, definitely captures people's attention (Pinheiro, Barros, Dias, & Kotz, 2017). We encourage facilitators to welcome playfulness and laugh with their groups whenever appropriate through images, humorous exchanges, or cartoons. Cathy Thorne of "Everyday People Cartoons" publishes many fun examples of mindfulness cartoons. Research has shown that people tend to remember humorous information better (Strick, Holland, Van Baaren, & Knippenberg, 2010), and are more attracted to a humorous facilitator (Cooper, Kong, & Crossley, 2018). Laughter is also associated with improved relationships, intimacy, a deeper state of relaxation, enhanced performance and motivation, openness, and a number of physiological benefits such as activating the dopamine system of the brain (Savage, Lujan, Thipparthi, & DiCarlo, 2017). While the experience of mindfulness meditation itself does not involve laughter, the introductions and information about the exercises, some of the breathing practices, and discussions can occasionally include entertaining images, metaphors, comments, and ideas that will be amusing, incite

Box 3.3 Attention in Action

Stories are inspiring, such as the following from an unknown author: One day, a father of a very wealthy family took his son on a trip to the country for the purpose of showing his son how very poor people can be.... On the return from the trip, the father asked his son, "How was the trip?"

"It was great, Dad. I saw that we have one dog and they have four. We have a pool that reaches to the middle of our garden and they have a creek that has no end. Our patio reaches to the front yard and they have the whole horizon. We have a small piece of land to live on and they have fields that go beyond our sight. We have servants who serve us, but they serve others. We buy our food, but they grow theirs. We have walls around our property to protect us; they have friends to protect them."

With this the boy's father was speechless.

participants to come back, better remember the material, and feel bonded to their group. We encourage facilitators who have a sense of humor to express and incorporate their creative ideas, when relevant, at the beginning of the facilitation scripts.

"Thanks, Dad, for Showing Me How Poor We Are"

Participants of all ages are compelled to pay attention to stories. Stories give life and meaning to the driest theoretical material and allow participants to feel connected to the material, engaged, and intrigued. Some of the exercises in this book offer anecdotes in their introduction to help participants connect with the value and applicability of some practices. Stories also provide a transition between people's busy lives before they join the session and the mindfulness exercise. They offer an entertaining or captivating break from worries and allow participants to ease into a state of presence during the group experience. Facilitators can feel free to add to and enrich their session with relevant stories they read or that come from their own lives.

Summary

There are many ways to tap into the brain's attention systems—sparking curiosity, showing visual images, inducing discomfort, using humor, telling stories, etc. Though these strategies are interwoven in the exercises in the following chapters, we strongly encourage facilitators to expand on these strategies during their sessions and to add attention-grabbing aspects as appropriate. Again, it is important to tailor the experience to each specific group—try out the strategies in this chapter that are a good fit for your participants and that match your comfort level and facilitation style. The following chapters include mindfulness exercises that progressively increase in complexity and difficulty. Let's start with innovative breathing exercises, which are the perfect place to begin a mindfulness practice.

CHAPTER FOUR

Powerful and Short Breathing Exercises for Stressed, Anxious, or Distracted Minds

Breathing exercises can help us rebalance our body, oxygenate the brain, soothe agitation or worries, and focus our minds very quickly. When busy or stressed, people have very little time for mindfulness meditation, even though they may be in dire need of the mental clarity and inner peace it offers. This is the case for a number of people working long hours to meet stringent deadlines, or for emergency room doctors and nurses who have to quickly make life-altering decisions. For the majority of people, walking away from their tasks for 20 minutes to engage in any regular mindfulness practice does not seem feasible. This extreme busyness can also affect teachers who have to impart an unrealistically heavy curriculum to a large number of students, caregivers who juggle work and parenting obligations, or student-athletes who must balance long hours of training with academic requirements. Busyness makes it difficult for adults to pause, relax, and concentrate on one simple aspect of their body such as breathing. A similar effect is found with younger students who spend long hours in front of video games and then simply can't concentrate in class. In such situations, the quick 1–5-minute *active* breathing exercises described in what follows can dramatically transform someone's day. In fact, research has even shown that three 10-minute practices of active breathing exercises can enhance students' attention skills on tests given immediately after (Gorman & Gree, 2016).

Basic Physiology of Breathing

As mentioned before, breathing is one of the rare activities controlled by both the autonomic and voluntary nervous systems. The autonomic nervous system carries out all the basic vital functions independently of our awareness; it controls the heart, lungs, digestion, circulatory system, etc. It is divided into the sympathetic and parasympathetic nervous systems. The sympathetic nervous system prepares the body for action by increasing heart rate, blood pressure, muscle tone, and the production of various hormones such as cortisol in times of stress. The parasympathetic system does the exact opposite—it decreases heart rate, blood pressure, and muscle tension, helping the body relax, focus, and when appropriate, sleep.

During a cycle of breath, the sympathetic system is mobilized through inhalation, loading the body with oxygen. The parasympathetic system is activated when exhaling and relaxing. Breathing exercises meant to relax people often lengthen exhales and insert pauses in the respiratory cycle, while breathing exercises meant to energize people reduce the pause and slightly accelerate the intake of oxygen. Before manipulating the breath, it is paramount that facilitators know whether anyone in their audience has medical issues such as asthma or other conditions that would require getting a doctor's approval. If a participant has a heart or pulmonary condition, or is pregnant, it is strongly advised that they refrain from engaging in any of these exercises. In general, most forms of breathing exercises, when done well and with care, have a multitude of benefits for healthy participants and insert a peaceful pause of *being* in busy days.

The collection that follows includes original creations, which have been favorites in our program, and traditional *pranayama* practices from the Eastern world adapted to fit Westerners' overly busy minds. These 18 exercises comprise only a sample of the many ways breathing can be used to influence the body, heart, and mind. Discussion questions are provided for each of these exercises, but they are optional, and not included in the time allocated for the facilitation. Approximately 10–15 minutes should be added for a discussion if desired.

These active breathing practices can stand on their own at the beginning of an academic class, during a private therapy session, before an athletic training, or they can be combined with the other exercises described in this book. Unlike the Fascinating Body Parts chapter, which focuses on cultivating observation and awareness, most of the exercises in this section *manipulate* the breath to enhance relaxation, focus, or confidence. The intention here is to nudge the body, to gently alter the pace of breathing *without forcing it*. It is crucial to avoid the state of gasping for air. For this reason, all of the exercises are very brief, and kindness to our body is key. The intent is to quiet the sympathetic nervous system and to access an optimized level of functioning, clarity, coherence, and focus.

The exercises are listed in incremental order of difficulty, and build on one another. They can all be done in an individual or group setting, except for

"Laughing Rhythms," which is more effective and satisfying with a group, and "Whole versus Connected," which requires another participant. Facilitators may wish to practice how they will balance providing a breathing demonstration while verbally explaining the exercise, since it's difficult to do both at the same time.

The Five Basics

Words of wisdom: "Breathing was your first action when you came into this world, and will be the last when you leave it."—Thich Nhat Hanh

Intention: Instill awareness of the experience of breath in the body, and introduce the concept of consciously manipulating the breath in order to stabilize the mind.

Time: 2–5 minutes

Props: N/A

Overview

Facilitators can choose how much explanation they wish to share based on how long they intend the exercise to last. These short basic exercises introduce participants to multiple dimensions of breathing (pace, sequence, structure, pause, posture, and embodiment) and allow facilitators to evaluate and correct their mechanics, if necessary. Many people breathe from their chest—which is ineffective and conducive to anxiety—and need to learn to better mobilize their diaphragm before moving on to powerful exercises like the Two Blankets or Snow Globe featured later in this chapter. The basic exercises can be done seated, but it is much easier to single out the diaphragmatic movement when standing or lying down, since most other muscles are neutralized. The beginning of the facilitation script here is the same for the five introductory exercises, and facilitators simply choose one of them for their session. Some of these are well-known traditional yogi practices such as the double exhale, or the in nose, out alternate. Some are creative modifications of classic practices, such as "The Flag," where participants mentally focus on alternate nostril breathing *without* using fingers to physically block one side of their nose. Others are original creations or exercises based on scientific and clinical applications for people struggling with anxiety or focusing issues.

Facilitation

Breathing happens automatically, so we often take it for granted. Some people even live their entire life without noticing its cycle! Yet, when you think about it, it plays a crucial role! If you were dangling from a rope, and your life depended on it, would

you scan and observe it once in a while? "Breathing is your rope, between life and death" (Salzberg, 2010). *Some scientists even report that no two people breathe in the same way, and that the way we breathe has a great impact on our health and how long we live* (Smalley & Winston, 2010)!

Let's be curious and observe our breath for a few minutes. This will calm our minds and allow us to focus. This is hard to do at first because we are used to the body breathing on its own while our mind wanders. We will try to reverse that: we will attend carefully to our breathing and allow the body to loosely relax.

Before we begin, observe and rate your level of tension, or agitation, on a scale of 1 to 10. Now stand with your feet hip distance apart ... arms alongside your body and relaxed ... your back straight without creating unnecessary tension ... head above your shoulders. Close your eyes softly, try to relax and breathe normally, peacefully for a few seconds. Be aware of your body breathing in this space. Make sure you are breathing from your belly and not from your chest. Technically, your chest and shoulders should be almost still, as your most effective breathing is through your nose (not your mouth) and involves your lower abdomen, your belly. You can place your hands on your belly to feel it rise and fall, and after a few minutes, let them hang by your side, if you'd like.

Exercise 1: Simple to Double

When you're ready, inhale as usual and then slowly begin to elongate your exhale so that it becomes twice the length of your in-breath. You may mentally count, if you wish, such as inhale, 1, and exhale, 1, 2. Do that for a few cycles, without forcing. You don't want to get out of breath. See if you can naturally gravitate to longer, softer counts, such as inhale 1, 2, pause, exhale, 1, 2, 3, 4, again without forcing and getting out of breath. Do this for 1–2 more minutes at your own pace, before we conclude the exercise.

Exercise 2: In Nose, Out Alternate

You will now inhale through your nose and exhale through your mouth, then inhale through your nose and exhale through your nose. Repeat this pattern, concentrating on keeping your mind focused on the breath and alternating the type of exhale. We will do this for about 1–2 minutes. See if you can keep this rhythm without getting distracted and losing sight of the task for a couple more minutes, and then we will stop.

Exercise 3: Your Inner Cat

Continue breathing softly and at your next in-breath, bring your attention to your belly. Most people don't know that we have neurons (brain cells) in our gut. In fact, that is why there is so much written on the "gut feeling" and the "gut brain."

Our gut contains almost the same number of neuronal cells as there are in a small cat's brain! So we can technically put our hands on our belly and imagine a small cat sleeping there. Feel the warmth of that area ... feel each in-breath and out-breath creating a rising and falling movement ... feel the peacefulness that can exist there ... feel the vibration associated with living tissue ... it is different to touch a living creature than an inert object ... feel the life of the cells there ... and the trillions of good gut bacteria working for you! If you'd like, for the next, last minute, you can very softly stroke that area or massage it, very slowly, to not wake the cat, while still paying attention to the rise and fall of the breath!

Exercise 4: The Four Windows

Notice that you have several openings in your head, the nose and mouth in the front, and ears on each side; these can be imagined as windows! Let's pretend that you also have a small air hole, a hidden opening or window, in the back of your head. You now have at least one "window" on all four sides of your head, and they can all be utilized to metaphorically circulate fresh oxygen in the head. Imagine breathing in through your nose and exhaling through the back of your head. ... On your next inhale, breathe in through your right ear, and exhale through the left ... then breathe in through the back of your head and exhale through your nose ... and breathe in through your left ear and exhale through the right ... go back to breathing in through your nose and exhaling through the back of your head, and repeat at your own pace, going in the other direction, breathing in through your left ear ... for one more minute.

As a level two of the Four Windows exercise, facilitators can play a game where they randomly switch the direction of the rotation several times, and encourage the group to pay careful attention to make sure everyone ends at the same window. Adult participants love this challenge and definitely intensify their focus on the instructions, which are as follows: "*You will now track, on your own, which side of the head we are all breathing from. I will add the fun challenge of calling a reversal of directions here and there. We will all try to carefully follow all the switches and end at the same place. Here we go: "In ... Out, ... In ... Out, ... In ... Out ..., reverse, In ... Out ..., reverse, In ... Out ... In ... Out, In ... Out, reverse, In ...Out, reverse. Open your eyes. How many of you took your last in-breath through the left ear window? Great, we all succeeded at the challenge!*"

Exercise 5: The Flag

This exercise is about controlling the wandering mind by anchoring our focus on one aspect of active breathing. Focus your mind intently on inhaling through only one nostril at a time. After your next exhale, focus your mind on breathing in only through your left nostril,... then exhale as usual through your nose ... focus on inhaling only through your right nostril,... and then exhale as usual ... inhale only through your left nostril again,... and exhale normally ... inhale only through your right nostril ...and exhale ... keep going for five more complete, slow and full rounds, at your own pace. Don't worry if there is still some air being inhaled on the other side, again this is about controlling the mind's focus by using the breath. ...

Optional Discussion Questions

- *What was the difference between how you felt at the beginning and at the end?*
- *What did you discover about your breath?*
- *Did your mind wander a lot and could you bring it back kindly?*
- *What were you most able to focus on?*

The Quick Resets

Tree People

Words of wisdom: Humans are like trees of life animated by breath.

Intention: Introduce a simple mental exercise that keeps the mind focused on breathing, and is both calming and energizing.

Props: N/A for adults or teens. For children: straws, glue, cardboard, and foam balls are optional.

Time: 5–7 minutes

Overview

This exercise works best standing. Tree people breathing involves imagining that you are breathing in nutrients mostly through either your roots or your crown. Curiosity is induced by asking participants to notice what kind of tree person they prefer to be! Village A people breathe from roots under one foot, inhale nutrients (air) through capillaries all the way to their head, and exhale down the other side. Village B people breathe mostly from their crown and send air and nutrients downward.

Facilitation

Today we will imagine being a tree person inhaling nutrients from our roots or crown. You will be exposed to two different styles of tree people and asked afterward which one feels most like a fit for you—village A, from the roots up, or village B, from the crown downward.

Position your legs hip distance apart, allow your arms to relax alongside your body, close your eyes, and make sure that your weight is equally balanced on both of your feet. Notice any tension or stress in your body. Then, take a first deep breath to relax, and let go of all thoughts to focus on the present time, engaging in this brief amusing experiment.

Let's start with village A style (see Figure 4.1). Standing still and peacefully, imagine that you are an unusual tree-like creature and have roots under both of your feet. ... You are inhaling nutrients through the left foot, all the way to your head, and exhaling used air molecules down the other side, "out of" your right foot. ... Again, you are inhaling air from under your left foot that will travel up through capillaries or tube-like structures, all the way to your head, and then exhaling the residues down the other side of your body to be disposed of by the roots under your right foot. ... Now reverse the direction, breathing in from under your right foot, all the way to your head, and then exhaling down your left side. Repeat: up right foot, head, down left side. Continue at your own pace, alternating sides, and complete three to five cycles. ... Notice how comfortable you are ... (allow 1 minute).

After your next exhale, switch to village B style (see Figure 4.1) and inhale from above your head, as if you had a canopy in the air above you and are funneling nutrients downward, filling your upper body with nutrients, and then exhaling down both sides of your legs. ... Repeat three times at your own pace ... breathing from the top of your head, filling your upper body, and exhaling downward in both of your legs. ... Notice how comfortable this style is for you. ... After a few such breaths, remain still and breathe normally. Feel the difference in your body ... feel anchored to the ground and stable ... and keep your head held high in the air.

Optional Discussion Questions

- *Raise your hand if you preferred village A breathing. How about village B? Can you explain how different it felt and what led to your preference?*
- *Are we connected differently to our breathing when we imagine being trees?*
- *What sensations did you have while imagining the air traveling up and down?*
- *What was most satisfying about this exercise?*

Youth Variation

With any audience open to creativity, it is fun to label village A as Earth connected, and village B as Sky focused. The tree imagery can also be replaced by straw figures. With younger children, building a straw character or a tree can make a nice complementary art project. Simply tie two straws together with an elastic band, and glue a small foam ball head

Figure 4.1. Tree People: Village A Breathing (Left) and Village B Breathing (Right).

or canopy on top, then glue it to cardboard where roots can be drawn (or represented by cut elastic bands).

Tornadoes

Words of wisdom: Tornadoes—rapidly moving air—are the ultimate cleanser of human constructions, including physical, emotional, or mental states.

Intention: Help people quickly reset their bodies to a more peaceful state.

Time: 1–2 minutes

Props: N/A

Overview

Participants are asked to breathe deeply four times and to imagine that the air they inhale is twisting and churning rapidly all the way down each of their limbs, one after the other, capturing all the agitation and "hyper energy" in a cleansing way, and blowing it out and away. They can then feel as if they had found a peaceful place to rest in the body, as if in the eye of a tornado. This exercise was first described in Beaudoin and Taylor (2009) and has remained a popular quick exercise in many schools.

Facilitation

Let's take a minute to stand up and take some deep tornado breaths. When I have finished sharing the instructions for this exercise, we will all do it at the same time. You will breathe in, in a slightly deeper and faster pace than usual, and imagine that the air is actually twisting as a tornado, as it enters the nose and travels down the throat and to the lungs. Since the air we inhale travels from our nose to our lungs in tunnel-like passages like our throat (or the esophagus), it's easy to imagine the air swirling around. The nose can also move slightly and help create a vortex of movement from one side of the nostrils to the other.

Let's try it together, just one time for now. Close your eyes, take a deep breath, and feel your nose moving slightly from side to side, and the air twisting in all the way down to your lungs. When you exhale, imagine exhaling debris such as carbon dioxide molecules. Great first tornados, everyone!

Now we will take four more tornado breaths, one after the other, together as a group, and direct the air all the way to each of our limbs, one at a time. Given that this in-breath covers the whole length of the body, it is helpful to have salient markers in mind such as throat, lungs, knees, and feet. You want to send air all the way down to your toes and make sure that it's brushing the inside of all of your toes, to clean them of every ounce of tension, or hyper energy.

Let's start with a tornado breath toward the right leg, inhale deeply, past your throat, lungs, and knees, all the way down to all the toes of your right foot and exhale back up and out from your mouth. Now inhale a tornado toward your left foot, making sure everything in your toes is brushed by this fresh air, and exhale loudly … then send a tornado breath toward your right arm, all the way to your right hand and fingers, and exhale. One last time, inhale a tornado breath deeply and visualize the air going all the way down your left arm, hand, and fingers, and exhale. Resume breathing normally, feeling the cleansing, relaxing, and focusing effect of the fresh air. Notice that your body is more peaceful as if you had found the quiet eye of the tornado. There may be movement outside of this room, but inside we can be very still.

Optional Discussion Questions

- *How many of you were able to visualize or feel the swirling of air?*
- *What difference does it make to imagine moving air when we breathe in? Does it make it easier to focus on it?*
- *Did focusing on rapidly moving air over a specific body part help to disconnect from overthinking and center you back in the present time? At the end, did you feel as if you were in the eye of the tornado?*

Youth Variation

Young people, especially elementary school children, tend to really enjoy this exercise. It is an engaging concept with powerful imagery, and this helps children have a better idea of what breathing can feel like in their bodies.

Invisibility Cloak

Words of wisdom: "When everything is moving and shifting, the only way to counteract chaos is stillness."—Kristin Armstrong

Intention: Practice stillness.

Time: 2–5 minutes

Props: Chime

Overview

Invite participants to become as still as possible and make their breath invisible (without gasping for air), as if they needed to save energy, or as if they needed to be invisible in order to avoid being seen.

Facilitation

Let's take 2–3 minutes to practice invisibility! In nature, most animals, including humans, see other creatures only when they move. Well-respected teacher, monk, and author Thich Nhat Hanh (2015) even shares the story of soldiers entering a monastery in the complete darkness of night, thinking no one was there. When they lit candles, they were startled to discover 60 monks fully concentrated on their meditation and absolutely still, as statues, … the disconcerted soldiers didn't dare disturb them!

We will sit very still for only 2 minutes, so … make it worthwhile! We will try to slow our metabolism so much that we barely need to breathe, and the movement of the breath will become subtle and minimal. Remember that thinking takes a lot of oxygen, so the less you think, the less your body needs to breathe, and the more you feel invisible. I will stop talking soon to practice this with you, and ring the chime after 2 minutes of silent stillness. We will then listen to the fading sound of the chime for as long as possible before we move. So let's begin. Close your eyes, take one normal breath and exhale very slowly. … Try to become as still as the floor or the chair … merge with it. Feel the weight of gravity on your body, as if it was a cloak of stillness and invisibility … try to even slow down your heart rate … without forcing anything … just imagine your body is slowly becoming statue-like (sit for 2 minutes of stillness, then ring the chime; a few seconds after the chime sound has completely disappeared, invite people to open their eyes).

Optional Discussion Questions

- *Did you find stillness? How would you describe how different your body is now?*
- *How was it to make your breath invisible? What else did you slow down?*
- *Did you know you could be so still and statue-like?*

Youth Variation

Invisibility is exciting, especially if you associate it with Harry Potter's invisibility cloak; with young children, you can also bring small and light blankets that children can gently place over their bodies to pretend having an invisibility cloak. This exercise can be facilitated a few times with other metaphors and images such as going into hibernation or being a prey with a lion nearby.

Shaping Pauses: A Mystery

Words of wisdom: Oceans breathe waves, mountains breathe wind, humans breathe oxygen, and yet… all find peace in pauses.

Intention: Provide imagery that manipulates the breath and helps participants study different types of pauses.

Time: 5–10 minutes

Props: These illustrations (see Figure 4.2) should be shown to participants at the beginning of the exercise in order to help them visually understand the exercise.

Overview

Participants are invited to manipulate the length of their inhales, exhales, and pauses according to geometric shapes and to solve a mystery question: which pause is most relaxing: when lungs are full of air, or when they are empty?

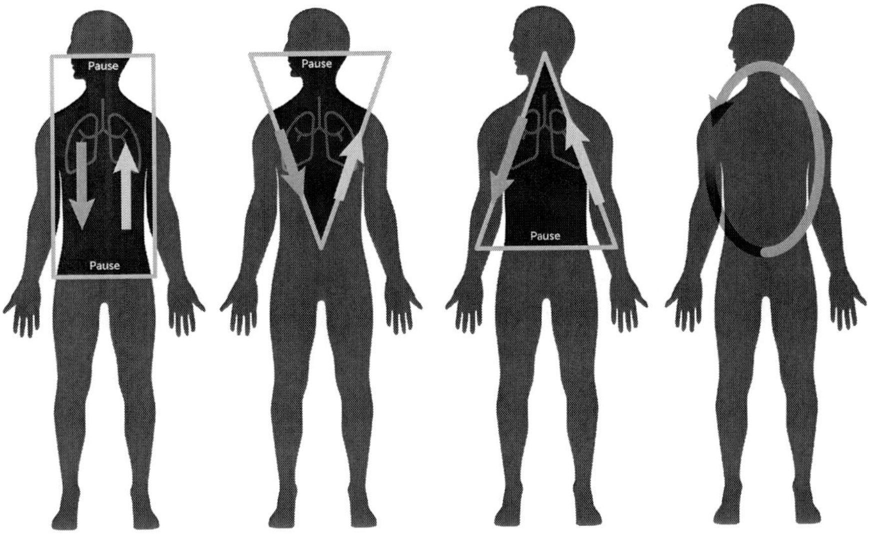

Figure 4.2. Breathing Patterns Can Be Guided By Different Geometric Shapes.

The duality of combining an action (modifying the breath) with a mental image (geometric figure) offers the advantage of fully capturing mental activity and redirecting it to present time sensations. It is very difficult for participants to accomplish this exercise while thinking of anything else. This exercise relies on traditional principles of *pranayama*, some of which were popularized and Westernized by Andrew Weils, including, for example, the four, seven, eight breath (inhale four counts, hold seven counts, and exhale eight counts) or box breathing (in three, hold three, exhale three, hold three). While four, seven, eight, and box breathing can be helpful, the geometric series outlined below adds a visual component, the possibility of experimenting with different rhythms, and a mystery question that helps people of all ages focus their minds on the task. The different shapes also increase the likelihood of finding a fit for participants' unique body needs.

Please note that the first three figures (square, triangle 1, and triangle 2) induce a state of relaxation, while the last (oval) brings participants back to a state of peaceful alertness, and ready to engage in a discussion or a mental task requiring focus. The reason for this distinction is that the first three shapes progressively increase the length of the pause between inhale and exhale, which means that there is temporarily less air exchange in the body, so carbon dioxide slightly builds up while oxygen slightly drops. This increases the amount of blood directed to the brain. The last geometric shape in the exercise, the oval, reduces the pause and replaces it with a constant yet very subtle movement of inhaling and exhaling that reinvigorates the body and increases the amount of oxygen available in the brain.

Facilitation

The exercise today involves mentally following the lines of imaginary geometric shapes floating about 2–3 inches above the breathing area of your body. These shapes will extend from the lowest part of your abdomen to the tip of your nose, as you can see in the following illustration (make sure everyone gets a good look). *You can place one hand under your belly button and the other on your chest to better feel the movement of air. You will experiment with adding, shifting, and removing pauses in your breathing cycle, and … solve a mystery! Which pause is more peaceful for you: when your breath is held in during certain shapes or when your lungs are empty? The answer to this question will become particularly visible when we do the triangle shapes. This exercise can be more relaxing lying down, but you can choose to remain seated if you'd like. So everyone close your eyes. …*

Let's start by noticing the air that flows in and out of our nostrils, with our mouth closed. Imagine the movement of air flowing upward and downward from the bottom of your abdomen to your nose. Notice the movement of air on the outside of your nose: the skin just below that area can sense air moving upward toward the nose on the in-breath and moving downward from the nose on the out-breath. Imagine that you could feel that movement on the surface of your body all the way to below your navel, as if the air was moving in a narrow corridor upward toward your nose and then downward toward your lower belly when you exhale. Take three to five breaths, slowly, while imagining this stream as a flexible string of air molecules gently moving up and down an imaginary line.

Now imagine that this one line is enlarged and transformed into a square, or a rectangle, about the width of your body, stretching out past your shoulders, all the way from your abdomen to your nose. Each side of the square will represent a different breathing activity—you will breathe in as you go up the left side, pause as you go across to the next corner, breathe out as you go down the right side, and pause again as you return to your starting corner. Let's try it.

You're breathing in, following one square side line upward, from your belly to your nose on a count of 1, 2, 3 … now holding your breath for a count of 1, 2, 3 as you cross over to the other side, now exhaling down to your belly for 1, 2, 3 on the other side of your body, and finally holding your breath again for a count of 1, 2, 3 and mentally crossing over to the other side as we saw in the illustration. Visualize the square you are creating with your mind. Each person is unique and may need to adjust to a count of 2 or a count of 4, whatever is needed to not overly force the breath and for this exercise to remain relaxing. Take a few breaths along the lines of this square or rectangle (if you are tall!). Air is moving up and down the side of your body, and the pauses are below your nose and below your belly button as your attention is crossing over. How do the pauses feel? Study the experience of pausing with your lungs empty after the exhale.

Now let's imagine that your square is losing some of its lower segment and becoming a triangle pointing down to the ground, with its tip at the bottom of your abdomen and its base just below your nose. Start at the tip of the triangle, at the center of your belly, and inhale. Move upward toward the base of the triangle—your in-breath lengthens to a count of maybe 5 or 6—then hold and mentally cross over under your nose to the other side of your body, with your lungs full but not overly so, for the same count of 5 or 6, and then exhale very slowly along the last side of the triangle, back down to your belly. The sides of your triangle do not need to be equal. Some people are more comfortable with an inhale of 5 counts, a hold of 6, and an exhale of 7. Again, whatever feels comfortable for you without getting out of breath and without forcing is the right way for you. Let's breathe along the lines of this triangle for a few cycles. Notice the sensation of a pause with your lungs full of air. …

Now on your next exhale, add a pause at the base of your abdomen, and let's reverse the triangle so that its base is at the bottom of your abdomen and its tip is at your nose. The inhale moves the air up to your nose, but there is no longer a pause there; you simply exhale downward, and then take a long pause as your attention mentally crosses over the width of your lower abdomen. … Notice the pause with your lungs empty, at the base of the triangle, at the base of your abdomen. Pay attention to how different it feels compared to lungs full. Do that a few times … at your own pace.

Our triangle will now be transformed into our final geometric figure: an oval. Imagine that your breathing pattern no longer has any angles or tips, and everything is becoming smooth. You can visualize the circular movement of throwing something in the air, having a minimal pause, and then gently circling back down. Or you can visualize an in-breath going up your spine and coming back down behind you. Or it can simply circle around your abdomen. Try to find what kind of oval image best fits your body right now. You are breathing in slowly and exhaling while minimizing the change of speed so that there is minimal slowing down at the end of your inhale and minimal acceleration while going to your exhale. The beginning and end of the breath morph into the other peacefully. Breathe along the lines of an oval for a few cycles, at your own pace, making sure not to force anything. Notice what it's like to have barely any pause.

When you're ready, let go of all geometric figures and allow your body to freely resume its normal breathing pattern.

Optional Discussion Questions

- *Were you able to solve the mystery of which pause is more peaceful for you? What did you discover about pauses?*
- *Were you all able to follow the lines of geometric figures while breathing?*
- *Was keeping the mental image of a figure helpful to sustain the focus on the breath?*
- *Which geometric figure felt the easiest to follow?* (This will vary for each person).
- *Which geometric figure felt the hardest to follow?*
- *What was your favorite figure and why?*

Youth Variation

When facilitating this exercise with young people, the illustration is usually necessary. Instructions on not getting out of breath may need to be repeated regularly.

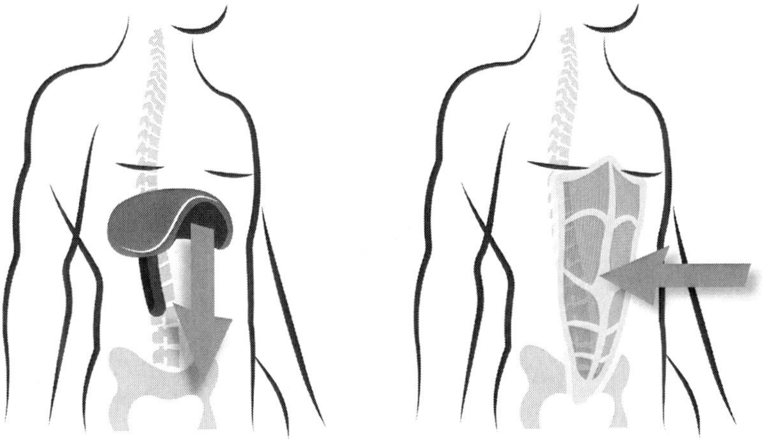

Figure 4.3. Inhale with the Diaphragm Moving Downward (Left). Exhale Fully Pushing the Abdominal Muscles toward the Spine (Right).

The Advanced

Two Blankets of Power

Words of wisdom: Monitor your breathing, because your breathing monitors you.

Intention: Reset the body.

Time: 3–6 minutes

Props: Image above and/or picture of the diaphragm and abdominal muscles

Overview

This very brief exercise is powerful enough to stop an anxiety attack or a moment of panic when done properly. It can be used in individual therapy or any group setting to help everyone be more grounded, present, and calm. It can be facilitated sitting or standing, as it involves slowly inhaling and exhaling to the very maximum of our abilities, by intentionally contracting the muscles involved.

This exercise is partially inspired by the traditional *kapalbhati* or *kapalabhati*, where people expel air forcefully by contracting abdominal muscles. Intensifying the contraction of muscles involved in breathing offers the advantage of enhancing the expelling of carbon dioxide from the lungs. This exercise can also be enriched with an ocean breath exhale, discussed later in this chapter. Make sure participants *never* push outward, but rather only inward or downward. Also, as mentioned earlier, participants who are pregnant or have a health condition should refrain from doing this exercise.

Facilitation

The brief breathing exercise we will explore today can reset your body very quickly in a moment of anxiety or panic. It uses powerful muscles: the diaphragm and the abdominal sheets.

The diaphragm is a dome-shaped muscle just under your rib cage that pushes all your abdominal organs downward when you inhale. This action creates a vacuum that sucks air into your lungs. The diaphragm can be metaphorically seen as a blanket, more or less parallel to the ground (when we are standing), that moves downward and compresses everything so there is room for fresh air. You can visualize that it has four corners, two in your front side and two in your back, and that you are intentionally pushing all four corners downward to their limit.

The abdominal muscles are in the front of your abdomen; there are three and they form a vertical wall or a sheet that covers your belly. They are generally perpendicular to your diaphragm.

The exercise involves alternating between imagining the four corners of your "blanket-diaphragm" pushing all the way down to your waist during the inhale, and imagining the four corners of your abdominal muscles and your navel pushing inward to the maximum of your ability on the exhale (see Figure 4.3). *Imagine trying to get your navel to touch your spine. Let's try each one of these alone at first. First, inhale all the way, pushing your diaphragm down toward your pelvis, feeling its four corners. Do this again with your eyes closed, just focusing on inhaling all the way down, without lifting your shoulders; just your abdomen is working. Now relax and breathe normally. Next, let's practice the exhale alone. Inhale as usual, then exhale, pushing your abdominal muscles inward, imagining your navel touching your spine and the four corners of this blanket crushing everything inward toward your back. Do this again. Relax. Now let's combine both.*

You can do this breath cycle a few times slowly (emphasize slowly), *and for most people this is very calming, especially if you connect with and notice the power of these muscles. Let's give it another try, slowly. Close your eyes ... inhale, down; exhale, back; in, down; exhale, back; in, down; exhale, back. ...One last time ... inhale, down; exhale, back. Breathe normally and open your eyes.*

Optional Discussion Questions

- *Was everyone able to visualize and feel the four corners of their "blanket muscles" pushing down during the inhale and back on the exhale?*

- *After some practice, many people describe their experience of this breathing exercise as empowering—has anyone felt this after this brief introduction?*
- *Can you think of situations in your life where you would benefit from using this quick powerful breathing practice? For example, some people use this in sports, to calm themselves and warm up, others use it when they face a highly stressful situation.*

Youth Variation

With young children, you may choose to do this for only two or three times at first, and add the possibility of visualizing a certain color, texture, and design for their inner blankets!

Wisdom Candles

Words of wisdom: "Just a single candle can both defy and define the darkness."—Anne Frank

Intention: Slow down an agitated mind and enter relaxation or sleep.

Time: 5–10 minutes

Props: Real candles can be a treat for all age groups but are not necessary. They require consideration of fire precautions and safety. Photos of people blowing candles can be helpful for children to notice the position of the mouth, but are optional.

Overview

Participants will progressively blow an increasing number of imaginary candles, while counting backward. The more they can blow, the calmer and therefore the "wiser" they become! This is so effective to calm the mind and body that a very basic version of this practice, called Pursed Lip Breathing (PLB), is used for people with asthma and chronic pulmonary diseases. It is modified here, adapted, and transformed into a fun exercise without losing its effectiveness.

Facilitation

Has anyone noticed how pleasant and satisfying it usually is to blow out birthday candles? As discussed before in other exercises, exhaling is relaxing to the human mind and body as it activates a special part of our nervous system. In fact, the more we exhale slowly, the quieter we can become IF, only IF we don't force it too much. It's the difference between nudging our breath to slow down versus overly containing it.

We will do an exercise where we practice exhaling with pursed lips, in tiny increments, as if we were blowing out an increasingly larger number of candles. Exhaling slowly with our lips in a pursed position opens up the airways in a unique way and prolongs exhalation. Of course, the more candles we can blow out, without straining, the calmer and wiser we become! Let me demonstrate how to do this. I will take a moderate inhale through my nose, with my mouth closed, and then exhale through my pursed lips, a small amount of air at a time, making sure that I'm saving enough to blow out "all my candles!"

Level 1

We will do three sets, so make sure to stop anytime this seems like it's going beyond your current capacity, or adjust the numbers. We will first count backward from 10 to 1, then 20 to 1, then 30 to 1. We will take a normal breath between each set. I'm fine with you completing a 12 to 1 count, then 15 to 1, and 18 to 1, if that's what your body can do today. The intention is to relax your own unique body and do what is helpful to soothe it, not to win a candle competition! I will not ask how many candles you each blew out! Try to feel some joy as you are doing this, after all you are blowing out candles, which is fun, even if they are imaginary! Let's start. Take a moderate inhale, purse your lips, and mentally count 10 to 1 as you gently pace yourself and blow candles. 10, 9, 8, 7, 6, 5, 4, 3, 2, 1. ... Breath normally. ... Let's do our second round, which I will do with you so you can count on your own.

Level 2

Level 2 should be a follow-up lesson; it could be too much to do this six times.

We were so successful with blowing out 30 candles last time that we can try to increase our age of wisdom! Let's see if we can start with 30 and then move up to blowing out 35–40 candles, while counting backward from 35 or 40 to 1! Then we'll breathe normally for one round and try counting from 45 or 50 to 1, and if that's still easy for some, we can end with a 60 to 1 count. Respect your body and don't force it. Your ability to blow out many candles can vary from day to day depending on how relaxed and rested you are. It will also vary depending on your age, health, physical fitness, and level of stress. It is a challenging exercise to do when you are feeling anxious, but can be very powerful in calming you down once you get the hang of it.

Let's try it. I will do the gentle blowing out candles with you and keep count in my mind, but it works best if you mentally count backward for yourself as well, to avoid your mind wandering. Begin by taking a normal nose breath. ... Now all together, let's breathe in through our nose slightly more than usual, pucker our mouth, and slowly start blowing out candles. ... (30, 29, 28, 27, 26, 25, 24, 23,

22, 21 …). … Now let's increase to 40 … (facilitator can go as high as suitable for most of the audience).

Optional Discussion Questions

- *How hard was it to blow out many candles?*
- *Were you surprised by the progress you made as this exercise unfolded?*
- *Did you notice the effect on your body?*
- *Did you feel a little wisdom sinking in as you blew out more candles?!*

Youth Variation

In order to help children connect with the experience of blowing out candles, it can be helpful to begin the exercise by asking children to remember the last time they blew out a candle, and even look at photos of the action. If a child has never blown out a candle, you can ask them to envision a time they saw it in a TV show or a movie, and practice the pursed lips breathing as a group.

Internal Snow Globe

Words of wisdom: Each in-breath invigorates roughly 3,720,000,000,000 cells in the body, creating an internal swirl of activity, much like in a snow globe.

Figure 4.4. Double Breath Triggers a Snow Globe–like Experience.

Intention: Explore a form of breath that alters our embodied sensations and creates an energizing experience of inner tingling.

Time: 10–20 minutes

Props: Optional snow globe to shake and watch the slow movement of particles as a demonstration

Overview

This exercise can be done only with people able to engage in diaphragmatic breathing. Participants are invited to inhale twice in a row and then exhale twice in a row in a rhythm that is very satisfying, energizing, and soothing. You can even use words to create the rhythm, such as "in, in, out, out." This is not done in an overly slow or fast way, but rather at the normal speed of speech. This exercise is adapted from the teachings of Paramhansa Yogananda and his direct disciple Swami Kriyananda.

Since this may create a small amount of temporary dizziness, it is best to facilitate it sitting or kneeling. Also, as mentioned earlier, participants who are pregnant or have a health condition should refrain from doing this more advanced exercise.

Facilitation

We will do a fun and energizing breathing exercise. We will create a rhythm with our breath by taking two inhales in a row, through our nose, and then exhaling twice in a row, preferably through the nose as well, although through the mouth is acceptable. We will follow the breathing rhythm "in, in, out, out." On the in-breaths, we will feel the swelling of the air in our abdomen during the first in-breath, and in our chest during the second. Another way to represent this rhythm is to think "belly, chest, out, out." This exercise intensifies both inhales and exhales, so that we are breathing in more air than usual and balancing this with a deliberate action of pushing the air out, twice in a row. The goal of this exercise is to create a little bit of temporary dizziness, which some people believe means that you are saturating your blood with oxygen and are energized. A nice way to think about this experience is to imagine that you are a snow globe, with peaceful, moving, sparkling molecules of oxygen floating in your body, which is mostly made of water (see Figure 4.4). This metaphor works well because about 60% of the adult human body is water, and some of our crucial organs contain even more. The brain and heart, for example, contain an estimated 73% water, our lungs about 83%, and our muscles about 79%.

The rhythmic "in, in, out, out" can be metaphorically seen as the breath movement "shaking" our inner snow globe. After a series of anywhere between

5 and 30 cycles, depending on your fitness and tolerance, you'll usually start feeling slightly dizzy. Please feel free to stop either at the very first sign of dizziness, or if you are comfortable with the experience, you can take a few more cycles to intensify it slightly. Each person will stop on their own, when it is best for their own unique bodies. Once you stop, remain in stillness for a few minutes, and notice that you do not need to breathe. Do not force anything; when your body wants to breathe, follow its lead, but you may not need to do so for a little while, which is often a fascinating experience. You become as immobile as everything around you and can just enjoy yourself as a snow globe. Observe the gently moving vibrations or tingling sensations everywhere inside of you. Notice where in your snow globe there is a sensation of movement and where there is stillness. Observe and enjoy! So let's start! Sit straight and make sure you engage your diaphragm. Let's begin. ... In, in, out, out. ... In, in, out, out. ...

Optional Discussion Questions

- *How many of you felt like a snow globe or felt a slight dizziness after the double breaths?*
- *How would you describe how you felt?*
- *Did you like the experience of being energized and not needing to breathe for some time?*
- *What was it like to be as still as everything around you?*

Youth Variation

Please teach this exercise to children only if you feel they are mature enough to engage in this practice responsibly, are able to consistently engage in diaphragmatic breathing, have learned all the other levels, and do not have health issues such as asthma. It is also essential to help them understand ahead of time that the lightheadedness will pass; it is not a sign of sickness, and it will be replaced by a satisfying experience of being both mentally calm and energized. Emphasize that this exercise has pleasant outcomes if we don't do too many. As with everything, an excess of any valuable activity can have negative effects. When pushed to the extreme or beyond someone's limit, this exercise can give a slight headache, which will eventually pass but is highly avoidable when people listen to their bodies.

Bubble Home

Words of wisdom: Just as every minute of erosion subtly shapes the river's banks in profound ways, each breath sculpt a micro-world inside and outside of you.

Figure 4.5. Bubble Breath.

Intention: Expand our field of awareness of the space and objects physically around us, and develop our ability to surround ourselves with a peaceful bubble (see Figure 4.5).

Time: 20–30 minutes

Props: Chairs to sit in, preferably spaced by 3–4 feet if possible

Overview

In our day-to-day life, our awareness of the space around us fluctuates and meanders based on what attracts the attention systems of the brain. Most people end up becoming oblivious to a large number of objects or people, which we take for granted. In this exercise, we will control our awareness by focusing on the space around us as if we were in the middle of a bubble, which will grow in size three times and will include an increasing number of elements from our *real* environment. The bubble home meditation is wonderful because it is always different wherever you are. It does not focus on *imagining* a safe place, like many other known exercises, but rather on truly perceiving and taking notice of what is physically around you.

Facilitation

Let's do a quick and fun little test! Close your eyes, and check how much of your surroundings you can clearly remember visually. For example, who's beside you? What is the color of the floor or the type of ceiling? How much do you actually notice of what's physically around you? Our attention will gravitate toward certain striking features and can easily become oblivious to so many other objects and people. Open your eyes and look around; fill your mental image with the information that was missing. Ideally, your mind and attention will dwell in the same place as your body, in the present time and space. As Jon Kabat-Zinn states: "Wherever you go, there you are."

Today, we will engage in an interesting experiment called the Bubble Home meditation. It consists of sitting with your eyes closed and imagining that you are creating a protective bubble home around you. You will breathe in normally, but when you breathe out, you will slowly blow a large bubble that will encircle you. You will be floating in the middle, as a yolk in the middle of an egg, and we will progressively increase the size of your bubble three times. I will give you some suggestions as to the size of your growing bubble, but feel free to adjust the size to something that is comfortable to you. Not everybody is comfortable with the same size of space around them, and it is important to respect your limits.

So let's get started. Sit comfortably and make sure your posture is erect, with your hands on your lap. Take another 20 seconds with your eyes open to observe again what is in your physical surrounding. You will need to remember these objects and many other details. Now close your eyes. Take a few normal breaths. ... When you are ready, on your next exhale, gently blow as if inflating a bubble around you. ... Do this three times, pursing your lips together to physically blow air, with a gentle sound, until you visualize yourself in the middle of a bubble of space, about 5 to 8 feet in diameter. Without opening your eyes, start remembering and visualizing what is truly in your physical space right now. Mentally review all the items that luckily ended up in your current bubble home. Become aware of the chair underneath you, the piece of floor, the space full of air, and any other objects or person in your sphere. This is your space right now; ...you can breathe in its air and exhale joy to fill your "bubble home." Keep your awareness on your bubble and all the items physically inside of it ... enjoy this time, as we will soon expand your bubble home. Relish this precious moment in this cozy space... Make sure your mind is not drifting into imagining or changing the space... Stick to your awareness of what is physically here...

When you're ready, inhale deeply and exhale through your mouth, slowly blowing air and increasing the size of your bubble. Do this three times, each time adding air in your bubble, with pursed lips, and making a gentle sound. Feel the air come out of your mouth as you are slowly blowing and increase your bubble to about 10 to 12 feet in diameter. You now have a greater amount of space around you; your bubble has been renovated! Observe your new home. As you are breathing in peacefully and joyfully, take notice of everything that is now inside your bubble of space. Do you remember what's in this space for 10–15 feet? All of the boundaries have changed, so there is much to notice; study your home, inch by inch, remembering in your mind's eye what now takes space in your home... If you don't know what's on the other side of this room, just imagine empty space... Your bubble now contains elements that are below the floor, ...it may include other people, who are visiting your space or coexisting peacefully, ...and it may include other objects. Take notice of every inch of your new space, ... discover what it now includes. Maybe it includes a portion of the wall... or some elements of the outside world; make sure you take notice of what is now above ... and behind you. Become aware of everything on each side of you three-dimensionally ... and continue to inhale, in a relaxed way, and breathe out joy in your bubble. Enjoy this new bubble home, with its real physical objects, as we will soon renovate and expand it.

When you are ready, we will expand our bubble one last time. On your next exhale, blow air gently through your mouth to increase the size of your bubble, and add another 10 feet to its diameter. Do this three times. Your bubble might now include a portion of the sky, and maybe some of the trees and flowers outside this room... It might include some of the earth below our feet, with all forms of peaceful miniature creatures contributing to the stability of our ecosystem... It may include other people who are all seeking the same inner peace and happiness in their own unique way... Be aware of the space around you and its details, ... and observe the weather of your bubble... When you are ready, feel free to adjust the size of your bubble to a space that is most comfortable for you; some people like to shrink their bubble, while others prefer to expand it further. Adjust your boundaries in a way that feels right for you today, just now; enjoy the size of that perfectly comfy bubble for a few seconds before we wrap up this exercise...

Make sure to inhale and exhale joy, peace, and love in your space, surrounding yourself with well-being. ... I will now slowly count backward from 3 to 1, and then we'll open our eyes feeling refreshed. 3,... 2,... 1. ... When you're ready, open your eyes. ... And look around you at the real physical space and its many objects.

Optional Discussion Questions

- *What was it like to surround yourself with a bubble?*
- *Did you become aware of items around you that you hadn't really paid attention to?*
- *Was it easy to expand your bubble?*
- *Which bubble size was most comfortable?*

Youth Variation

With children, you may consider inviting them to mentally decorate their bubbles with different imaginary objects at the very end, but this is optional as there is great value in just being aware of what simply exists in the real space and practicing pure observation.

Fun Collectives

Ocean Harmony

Words of wisdom: Dwell in the ocean of life, not on its occasional reef.

Intention: Engage the body in a controlled exhalation that is very relaxing and evokes a fun group experience of the ocean.

Time: 10–20 minutes

Props: N/A. With children, a recording of waves slowly and gently crashing on the shore can be fun to listen to during the introduction, and it can inspire children to recreate the sound on their own afterward.

Overview

This is adapted from the traditional *ujjayi* breath and has been used for many centuries in the Eastern world to balance the mind and settle agitation or worries. It is very pleasant, quite simple, and doesn't need much explanation other than "breathe in deeply, and exhale slowly while restricting the air in your throat and making a wave sound." Longer explanations are included here in case facilitators face a participant who struggles with grasping this exercise. Level 1 describes the traditional method and Level 2 describes a very lovely adaptation and innovative group experience developed in our program. If Level 2 is facilitated, allow time for sharing. People of all ages really enjoy the harmony and are delighted by the experience.

Facilitation

Level 1

We will take a couple of minutes to play with our breathing in a very relaxing way and contract some muscles we seldom pay attention to. Let's start by doing a few chin tucks. Gently try to pull your head straight back, as if it were gliding on a rail, while keeping your chin down. Place your hands on each side of your throat, and feel those muscles contract. Now relax your head, take a deeper than usual breath, and then, with your lips sealed, exhale while gently constricting your throat with those same muscles. You can exhale through your nose, or through your mouth for a more distinct sound. This contraction results in a sound akin to a wave crashing softly on the shore of a beach. This could also sound like a sigh of someone who is grumpy, but it is deeper and soothing, and—of course—more positive! Let's do this together. Notice how it mimics the sound of waves. We will do this breath four or five times—go at your own pace, and feel free to alternate exhaling through the mouth or nose to feel the difference.

Level 2

Now that everyone understands how to engage in the ocean breath, we will use that to simulate a three-dimensional auditory experience of the beach. How many of you enjoy going to the beach? Raise your hand. Wonderful! Has anyone meditated at the beach? If you have, you might have noticed a number of different sounds associated with waves crashing. You might also have noticed that waves are usually not crashing at the same time along the length of the beach because of the irregular ocean floor. This creates a harmony of wave sounds falling and receding one after the other. We will recreate this harmony by separating into three groups, and each group will begin its ocean breath a few seconds apart, creating an impression of moving waves in the room. We will do this about three to five times and I will cue your group when to start each time. I may even vary the speed of the harmony, so pay attention! You are free to end your ocean breath when you're out of air and to inhale on your own, but hold the air in until I point at your group to exhale through your mouth. People on the left here will form group one, people in the middle form group two, and those of you over there will form group three.

To start, everyone will take a deep breath in at the same time and will let it out only when I point at your group. It may take us a round or two to get in sync but we will get there! So everyone stand tall. On the count of three: 1, 2, 3 … inhale … (point at group one to exhale, then at group two, and finally group three, and repeat at a different pace).

Optional Discussion Questions

Note: Discussion recommended if facilitating Level 2.

- *How many of you succeeded in making sounds similar to waves, using your throat muscles?*
- *How does your body feel now, after this relaxing breath?*
- *What did you most enjoy about the beach harmony we created?*
- *How would people respond differently to challenges if everyone kept this relaxed state with them throughout the day?*

Youth Variation

Give children a longer set of cycles, as it may take a few minutes to practice your orchestra conduction skills and for the harmony to truly emerge.

A Humming Colony

Words of wisdom: The world contains 7,099 languages, and only one is common to all humans, yet rarely shared: humming.

Intention: Feel the very relaxing movement created by our vocal chords while humming, and the extent to which the vibration travels to our throat, head, and chest.

Time: 10–15 minutes

Props: N/A

Overview

The original humming breath was traditionally called *brahmari pranayama* in Sanskrit. It was created to lengthen exhales and to intensify sensations in the breath. The vibrations can be very soothing to a tense, busy mind. Weitzberg and Lundberg (2002) demonstrated that humming actually triggers beneficial physiological reactions in people. This study revealed a 15-fold increase in the release of nitric oxide in the respiratory system, a special substance that increases blood flow and facilitates the uptake of oxygen. Humming seems to offer benefits on many levels, such as increased joy, and is worth the experiment. Participants can practice humming in any position, sitting, standing, or lying down, but it is preferable on an empty stomach. Four sets of hums are facilitated with different foci: the first focuses on the vocal chords themselves, the second on feeling the vibrations travel, and the last two on becoming aware of the entire group humming in unison, like a colony of bees buzzing. It is unique and special to share this experience with a group.

Facilitation

Level 1

Few people know that the simple act of humming offers many health benefits such as relaxation, improved blood flow, and an increased uptake of oxygen. It also lengthens your exhale, which is automatically relaxing, and intensifies interesting sensations in your breath, which makes it easier to focus on it. The vibrations affect our facial and neck muscles in a way similar to a gentle massage, and some people report that it can reduce tension headaches. Interestingly, you have two sets of vocal chords that vibrate when air goes through your larynx (your "voice box"). Men and women have different voices and pitches because their vocal chords are of different lengths. Men's vocal chords are 17–21 mm long, while women's vocal chords are 11–15 mm long. Children's vocal chords are shorter—at birth, they are 2.5–3.0 mm and are located higher up in the neck (by the first cervical). Throughout childhood, they progressively descend down to the sixth or seventh cervical until they reach their adult length during adolescence (Prakash & Johnny, 2015). *Study your experience of humming; it is quite fascinating to feel what these vocal chords can do.*

We will briefly hum four times together as a group. Since you will be covering your ears when we start and will not be able to hear me, pay careful attention to the instructions I'm about to share. Your initial focus will center on the vocal chords, then expand to the neck area during the second hum, allowing you to notice how far the vibrations spread. For the last two rounds, I invite you to soak in the experience of being in a room full of hummers—it may sound like a group of bumblebees! Whichever way you hum will be fine; don't try too hard to remember the details of the instructions. Focus instead on whatever experience arises out of this experiment. When we all stop, we will enjoy 30 seconds of silence to feel the difference between vibration and stillness.

So let's all close our eyes, seal our lips softly, take a deep breath, cover our ears, and begin to hum at our own pace. (The facilitator loudly begins to hum).

Level 2

Everyone enjoyed last week's humming so much that we will do it again, slightly differently. We will do a bumblebee breath for four more rounds, but this time we will move our facial muscles in different positions. This will offer the benefit of relaxing tight facial muscles. It will also modify the humming sound in very interesting ways.

We will first embody a happily humming and buzzing bee with a smile on our face; then for the second exhale, we'll make a grumpy, unhappy face with our lips arched downward and hum. The third hum will be a nervous buzzing sound as if we were scared of something and said "yikes," stretching our mouths toward our ears and pulling away from something frightening, and the last hum can be whichever sound or facial experiment you wish to conduct while humming. Turning your head from side to side while humming gives your buzzing a zooming feeling, which can be quite fun. If you notice that one side of your neck is tighter and doesn't vibrate as much, try to intensify the vibrations there.

To recap, we will smile, frown, stretch our mouths toward our ears, and experiment freely. With each of these expressions, I encourage you to pay attention to your own inner sensations of the vibrations, sounds, and experience of being surrounded by different tones of buzzing sounds and auditory vibrations. So take a deep breath, and here we go. …

Optional Discussion Questions

- *How many of you enjoyed humming? Did you feel the vibrations?*
- *What did you notice in particular?*
- *How far up and down in your body could you feel vibrations?*
- *Were both sides of your head and neck equally relaxed, or did you discover some hidden tensions?*
- *Did moving your facial muscles in different positions affect the sound?*
- *What was it like to be part of a humming, vibrating group?*

Youth Variation

This exercise is well loved by children, and they could happily engage in more than four iterations. The facilitator may wish to allow five or six humming breaths with an excited group rather than attempt to control and end the exercise before children are content with the full opportunity to live this. With adolescents, this exercise will work well only if the group is safe and if there is a real likelihood of everyone doing it. In schools where bullying is a problem and students do not take risks, this exercise may be premature.

Laughing Rhythms

Words of wisdom: "The most wasted of all days is one without laughter."—E. E. Cummings

Intention: Help participants notice their breath during laughter, be an observer of the embodied process of laughing, and share the utmost enjoyable experience of laughing with a group.

Time: 5–10 minutes

Props: Usually not necessary, although with some groups, images of people laughing can be very inspiring and facilitate laughter. A meditation bell can be useful to end the exercise, but facilitators can also clap their hands if one is not available.

Overview

A number of human expressions, such as sighing and laughing, have valuable physiological effects on the body, as discussed earlier in this book. While we tend to experience them passively when they occur, it is also possible to initiate those ways of breathing voluntarily. Participants are invited to notice their level of energy before the exercise and afterward. Facilitators are invited to extend a higher level of enthusiasm in this exercise to really set the stage for genuine experiences of mirth.

Facilitation

Take notice of how your body is feeling right now, and how much energy you have. Give it a number on a scale of 1–10—I will ask you to notice the difference at the end of our exercise. We've experimented with various forms of breathing, but we haven't yet explored two forms of exhaling that happen naturally. Can you guess what they are? (facilitator takes guesses from participants). *Yes, sighing and laughing! Both of these expressions increase our intake of oxygen. Laughing has additional effects such as reducing stress, boosting our immune system, and protecting our heart—it may even help people live longer! Some people say, "Laughter is a form of internal jogging. It moves your internal organs around" (Norman Cousins). Others say, "Laughter is an instant vacation" (Milton Berle).*

We'll practice a voluntary version of these expressions by always taking only one long inhale but progressively increasing the number of "beats" in our exhale. The rhythm can almost feel like running down a staircase (facilitator demonstrates laughing and contracting the abdominal muscles several times, making a "ha!" sound, almost a whisper at first and progressively louder). *Before concluding the exercise, you will have a mystery question to answer: how many "ha!" sounds of laughter can you actually do in one exhale? I will let you know when to count your "ha." At the very end, I will ring a meditation bell (or clap my hands) to signal a pause of silence for 10–15 seconds. This silence and stillness is crucial to feel the difference in our bodies; you don't want to miss that!*

Let's give it a try, and remember it has to be slow and progressive to be fun. Take a slightly longer inhale ... and then whisper a gentle single "haaa" sound; now let's inhale deeply and exhale only twice, with a sound, "Ha! Ha!" Now inhale deeply and really laugh by exhaling three times, louder, "Ha! Ha! Ha!" Now inhale deeply and count how many smiling "Ha! Ha!" sounds you can actually do in one exhale. Repeat one last time and freely enjoy the sound of your laughter with as many "Ha" sounds as you'd like! (When most people have stopped laughing, the facilitator rings a meditation bell or claps, and facilitates 10–20 seconds of quiet).

Optional Discussion Questions

- *What was the difference in your body and energy level after a few laughs?*
- *How did you experience the simulated laughter?*
- *Had you ever noticed how you were breathing during a sigh or laughter before this exercise?*
- *What did you most enjoy about this experience?*
- *What is special about being in a group of people laughing together? Is it possible that it makes us feel a little more connected to one another?*
- *Do we better remember those moments that we laugh together versus just conversations?*

Youth Variation

Young people love this exercise and listen to the instructions quite well, including stopping at the end. This exercise requires a sense of safety to take the risk of spontaneously laughing in front of their peers. In some groups, it is easier if they are instructed to close their eyes and laugh internally. After the exercise, they can also be invited to draw their perception of their face or their experience of their body during laughter as an art project.

Challenges

Challenge Level 1: Whole versus Connected

Words of wisdom: Be one, and all—Inspired by "The Crippled-Who-Is-Whole," in *Eldest*, a book by Christopher Paolini (2005)

Intention: Experiment with the ability to be both an independent and interconnected being. This exercise is better suited for a group of people who know each other well and are comfortable with some closeness.

Time: 10–20 minutes

Props: N/A. Sitting in chairs is ideal.

Overview

Participants pair up with someone they feel comfortable with, and sit diagonally across from them (face to face can feel awkward). They will first center themselves and observe their own pace of breathing, and then shift from themselves to focus on their partner's abdomen. After some observation, they will both try to merge their pace of breathing. As a result, one person typically slows down a little and the other slightly accelerates. The merged breathing can last about five cycles. Participants then recenter themselves within their own natural pace of breathing. A popular version of this exercise, focusing on communication skills, was described in Beaudoin and Walden (1998).

Facilitation

As human beings, we are all similar and different. In particular, we are all breathing beings. We breathe at our own individual pace and also tend to enjoy engaging in an action at the same time as another. For example, we often greatly appreciate the surprise of yawning simultaneously, or unexpectedly uttering the same word in unison with someone. These moments trigger complicity, closeness, and amusement. Breathing in unison can trigger these same feelings. Since we are at the end of our series, we will experiment with a special exercise that emphasizes similarities and differences in breathing patterns. After I finish explaining the exercise, you will find a partner, preferably someone with whom you are comfortable (but it is not absolutely necessary). You will sit diagonally across from one another, at a comfortable distance from this person. Check if this distance is acceptable for both of you, and make sure that you are able to see each other's abdomen.

When we are all ready, I will cue you to close your eyes and start focusing on regular, peaceful diaphragmatic breathing. You can count your inhale and exhale pattern (for example, inhale 1, 2, 3 and exhale 3, 2, 1). After three to five rounds at your own pace, everyone will reopen their eyes and focus on the breathing rhythms of their partner.

Just observe at first, while keeping your own pace. This is difficult. After a cycle or two, you will slowly, ever so slowly, alter your breath pace to approach that of your partner, and try to reach a breathing pattern that you can both sustain for a few cycles. This means one of you will accelerate slightly and the other will slow down. It can often take two cycles to attain a joint pace since we're doing it slowly. Experience the joint breathing for about two to four cycles, nod to your partner to signal your disengagement, and then slowly go back to your own. When complete, you will close your eyes again and delight in the rhythm that fits your body perfectly, as a glove.

Discussion Questions

- *What were the differences between your own breathing versus that of your partner?*
- *How was it to share the same pace?*
- *Did you discover something that you hadn't noticed about your pace of breathing?*
- *Did you experience any appreciation when you came back to your own pace?*

Youth Variation

No changes are necessary for youth. This is a great exercise to do at home with a loved one or a child. It gives a brief glimpse into another person's experience of their body.

Challenge Level 2: The Power of Choice

Words of wisdom: Inner power unfolds from choosing the mind's focus rather than being captured by whatever is making the loudest noise, externally or internally.

Intention: Practice controlling your mind in spite of external noise.

Time: 5–10 minutes

Props: Audio recording and speaker. For an easier challenge, be prepared to play the audio recording of a meaningless soundtrack such as an unknown fundraiser event. For more advanced groups, play a documentary. A movie with suspense or the news would be too difficult for most people, and we want to ensure that everyone is successful. In case of doubt, choose a recording that will allow the person who struggles the most to succeed.

Overview

Ideally, participants sit or lie down in a circle and are encouraged to remember a favorite meditation, one that allows them the greatest grip over their minds. This may be a body part, an image, or the breath. After a minute or so, the facilitator will start playing a distracting audio recording, at a very low volume, in the middle of the circle. If people wished to decipher the words that are spoken, they would need to really perk their ears and pay attention. If participants cannot sit in a circle, please keep in mind that people closer to the recording will hear it more distinctly while those in the back will not. The distracting recording will be played for 1–2 minutes depending on skill level, and then participants can recenter themselves for 1 minute in silence. This exercise can have two levels with Level 1 being 1 minute at very low volume and Level 2 involving a slight increase in the volume.

Facilitation

Today we will test our ability to control our mind's focus. The mind is a "tool for survival," as Eckhart Tolle (2004) states, but sometimes we lose control over that tool and it controls us. This happens when we cannot stop thinking about the past or the future and are unable to focus our minds on the present time. So far, we have just practiced focusing the mind on the breath. Today, we will add a challenge by focusing on the breath with an audio distraction in the background. Most people's minds will seek to label the distraction because we are curious, and sometimes, when we tell the mind to not focus on the pink elephant in the room, it focuses on it even more. Remember that we are all capable of ignoring sounds (TV, music in the background, someone talking) in some situations. We have the ability to choose what enters our mind and our thoughts. This exercise is about practicing our mental control over our attention as opposed to it just happening randomly. Observing the inner battle associated with focusing the mind, in and of itself, can be very valuable.

I will give you 1–2 minutes to settle down in inner stillness, grab control of your mind and focus on your breath or a body part, whichever practice was successful for you in everything we have covered so far. After a minute or so, I will announce the beginning of the distracting recording. I will not tell you what the recording is about so that you can test your control. This is very difficult to do for everyone. You may find yourself craving to find out what the sound is about, or you may be able to resist that. Some people might know immediately what this is about. What matters is being able to go back to the focus on the breath or your senses. Whatever happens is fine; just observe in a peaceful, grateful way, and don't be hard on yourself if you do not succeed this first time. It is part of the practice to catch your mind wandering or being curious, and to bring it back gently to the present time—that is ultimately what strengthens your ability to control the mind.

So let us now begin. Find a comfortable position with your arms and legs uncrossed, and start focusing on your breath … find your center, your inner peace, and engage in a breathing practice that works best for you …(allow participants to breathe quietly for 1–2 minutes). *I will introduce the recording in a few seconds … intensify your hold on your mind, tell yourself it is a matter of great importance that you focus on your breath, as if you were about to lose your wallet or something crucial. Intensify your focus on an object of your choice; here we go* …(facilitator plays the recording for 1 minute, and then pauses recording). *Take one last minute to recenter yourself in silence.*

Discussion Questions

- *How many of you found this challenging, but succeeded for some portion of it?*
- *Which breathing exercise did you choose to control your mind and why do you think that one may be most helpful for you?*
- *What did you discover about your ability to resist distractions? About your ability to control your mind?*
- *Did anyone forget the distraction? How did you accomplish that?*

Youth Variation

This is a challenging exercise for young people, but it is nevertheless fun to try for a really short window of time (30 seconds). The expectation can be modified to just observing the battle for control, the curiosity part of the brain, or your own will to focus on what *you* want. A fun variation for teens would be to count backward from 100 to 1, while focusing on your breath, and not losing your count when the recording is played—otherwise you have to start over!

CHAPTER FIVE

Mindlight on Senses

Guiding the Mind to Better Focus

The activities described in this chapter are designed to assist people in developing focusing-related skills such as attention, memory, self-awareness, self-regulation, and pain management. This is accomplished by engaging in captivating exercises attending to sensory information (see Figure 5.1) and highlighting the effects of participants' mental choices.

Participants learn they can exert a great influence over what their minds focus on and therefore choose to reduce discomfort, on both a physical and an emotional level. As mentioned earlier, since everyone is always very interested in discovering ways to minimize discomfort, the application of these skills with pain management makes the project highly compelling to all age groups. With this gain in mind, people become genuinely interested, attentive, and excited to try their best. In the process, they develop many important skills such as a deepened ability to enter the state of stillness, listening with heightened attention, and connecting with their embodied sensations. The sessions are designed to build on one another, so we encourage facilitators to attempt to use them in order.

Each session of this project has an intriguing theoretical introduction, an exercise, a discussion, and a summary with an invitation to ponder and practice. Controlling the mind is metaphorically discussed as choosing where a light will focus and whether this light will zoom in on certain details, wander, or take in a greater perspective of an event.

Figure 5.1. Mindfulness Cultivates Our Ability to Tap into Our Senses.

Discovering Your "Mindlight" and Its Powerful Effect on Pain

Words of wisdom: Attention gives power to the object of its gaze.

Intention: Develop a relationship with the group, and establish a sense of intrigue and fascination for what the mind is and what it can accomplish in the face of discomfort.

Time: 30–40 minutes

Props: A headlight or a flashlight. Ordinary round office stickers, in the middle of which a small grain of millet, quinoa, or rice is affixed. Paper and pens for participant reflection are helpful, especially if the group is not 100% safe to make mistakes and experiment.

Overview

The mind is compared to a headlamp that has three modes: "zoom in," "wander," or "zoom out." As people sit still with their eyes closed, the facilitator affixes a sticker in the meaty part of the thumb of each person's hand. People are first invited to pay attention to the general sensations of having a sticker, and then asked to imagine how it would feel *IF* they were told the center of the sticker contained a substance that itched and burned a little. Just as having mosquitoes around gets a lot of people to feel somewhat itchy, the thought of a burning substance gets people of all ages to start feeling discomfort there. Brain-imaging research has demonstrated that expecting pain actually activates the insula, a brain structure heavily involved in this type of experience (Lorenz et al., 2005). As discussed earlier, emotional fear of pain generally activates the same area of the brain as actual pain, and it is easy to feel discomfort with the strange sensations of a sticker, especially when focusing intently on its center. After dwelling on the sensations, and for most of them, after imagining pain, participants are told their minds are powerful enough to create and eliminate pain, and encouraged to manage it. People are then slowly brought back out of the induction and invited to discuss the experience. Participants are then informed that we now have proof that their minds are *very powerful in a good way* and able to create or dissipate pain since there was, in actuality, no burning substance. It is of utmost importance that facilitators honor people's experiences. Words are carefully chosen so that people do not feel fooled by learning that there was in fact no substance, but rather empowered to realize that they have very powerful minds.

Facilitation

The mind can control pain in many ways. The key area of the brain that is activated for physical pain is the same as the area that recognizes emotional pain. What strategies have you used in the past to handle discomfort? Let's take the example of the last time you caught a flu. What helped reduce your misery? (List strategies on a board or big sheet of paper). *Most of the time, our mind is lured into focusing exclusively on the discomfort while it could focus on other things. What can it focus on?* (Write down their answers in an outlined drawing of the brain). *The mind is like a light with different settings* (actual headlamp demo). *Just as you might use a remote control to change what you are watching on a screen, you can choose channels, settings, or programs in your mind* (demonstrate using the light). *The three that we will explore are the:*

1. *"Zoom in": The mind focuses like a laser light, which helps us see a lot of details. In this setting, it can influence what we feel and do. Example: You can narrow it down and put all its power on one target such as changing sensations in our body. This "setting" takes practice, but it's worth it.*
2. *"Wander": The mind is not focused, and moves a lot more quickly than when on "zoom-in." Example: This setting is on when you listen but don't remember anything, or you go on vacation and can't remember what you've*

seen, or you're constantly switching the screen on your phone from texts to emails, games, YouTube, or Facebook.

3. *"Zoom out": The mind has a sweeping view that takes in a lot of different information and sees the big picture. Example: This setting is helpful when someone walks to a new place and remembers their way out, or when you leave this room and have a detailed picture of it in your mind.*

The mindlight is figuratively like a muscle that you can train. As most of you know, we have many muscles in our body. Those we use get stronger and those we don't use remain weak. Let's get started with a mind test and our first exercise in mind mastery. In a minute, we will all sit still, with our feet on the floor, and I will tell you what to do with your mindlight. I will ask questions, and I'd like you to NOT answer out loud, only mentally inside, in your mind. Then after a minute or so, I will walk around and place a sticker like this one in your hand (slowly show the top of the sticker clearly to everyone, not the quinoa seed). *So I need you to choose a hand, place it on your lap, and open it a little. You'll pay attention to the sensations around the sticker and follow very specific instructions. Try to listen well and not let your mind wander too much, otherwise you'll be lost at key moments of this exercise* (give out stickers to an assistant, if any).

Ready? Sit still with your feet on the floor and your eyes closed or relaxed. ... Make sure to put one hand on your lap and open it. ... Now take a deep breath in, and focus all your attention on the air going into your nose ... your throat ... and down into your lungs. ... Feel the air, notice its temperature ... notice if it's different than the temperature of your body ... and feel it going down your throat to your lungs. ... Now imagine the air going all the way into your arm, as if it was going down a long water slide. ... And bring your attention to your hand;... feel the skin of your hand. ... Let your attention examine the skin of your hand centimeter by centimeter and check if you feel any scratch anywhere. ... Focus on your hand for a few minutes while I affix a sticker on everyone's chosen hand.

Now bring your attention to the sticker. How does it feel to have a sticker in your hand? How would you describe the sensation of having a sticker there? Do you feel the glue, the stickiness ... what would your skin say if it could talk? See if your mind can trace the edges of the sticker clearly. ... Notice how foreign the sticker is in your hand, how your body can just accept to have it there, and be at peace if you decide so.

Now listen carefully; this will be the first part of this training. I will tell you something you don't expect, and it's really important that you don't move or say anything. Keep your eyes closed, and just focus on the sensations under the sticker. What if I told you that in the middle of the sticker, under the bump, there is a sub-

stance that makes your skin itch and burn just a little … try to feel this sensation in the middle of the sticker. … With your mindlight, just pay attention to the sensations in the middle of the sticker. … What do you feel? … What do you notice? … What's happening? … Some people feel it as a tickle, others as an itch, and others still as a warmer sensation. … Pay attention to these sensations and try to mentally put words to them. How would you describe these sensations?

Now remember that your mind is very powerful. When you feel something unpleasant, you can produce a shield for your skin. You can imagine your skin sweating and repelling the sticker with small drops of water. … Your skin can actually do that, and your mind can influence it to do that. Or imagine your skin producing something like a sunscreen that would protect you from harm. … Now focus intently on feeling good and protected. …The sticker is small and cannot harm you. … Take a deep breath and relax. … Feel the difference between your sticker hand and your other hand. How would you describe the difference? Okay, now we will all take three deep breaths together. I will count backward from 3 to 1, and when I reach 1, we will open our eyes and discuss the experience… 3 … 2… 1 … Open your eyes.

Discussion Questions

For all discussions, these questions are simply a jumping-off point and a way to trigger curiosity. Feel free to choose what works best for your group, and remind them that these questions are just to help them reflect on the experience. We do not expect them to always have an answer right then and there. For this exercise specifically, write a list of what the mind can do on a large piece of paper.

- *Can you describe more specifically what you felt on a piece of paper? Or: Raise a finger if you felt a little bit of a burning sensation under the sticker.*
- *Raise a finger if you didn't feel anything.*
- *I have a very good surprise for you: you have just proved that you have very powerful minds, because (gently) there was no burning substance in the sticker. It was just a quinoa seed. Remember that my words were: "What if I said there was a substance?" Since physical and emotional pain activate some of the same structures of the brain, just the thought, and especially the fear, of being in pain is sufficient to trigger the sensation for most people. Research on the brain has demonstrated that just expecting pain activates this area. Many of you might have noticed this phenomenon when there are a lot of mosquitoes around us and we suddenly feel itchy all over, even in the absence of bites. This exercise makes visible what your mind can do, and you were all successful. Congratulations! Just like the thousands of people who have*

participated in this exercise, your minds actually created these sensations and then practiced creating shields against them. You can remove the sticker and see the grain in its center; if you wish, you can keep the sticker as a reminder of your powerful mind.

- *What is it like to discover this feature of your mind? It can create pain and make problems bigger or smaller than they are in reality.*
- *How many of you were able to produce a shield or repel the sensations? What are the unique ways in which you did that for yourself?*

Summary

So today you discovered that your mind can be powerful; it can create and dissipate pain! Anything that the mind gives attention to usually grows in importance. Attention gives power to the object of its gaze. You've discovered how to find your mind's power and how to control sensations in your body. Between now and our next session, try to notice an opportunity to focus by using your zoom-in or zoom-out setting, and also, try to find a moment when you can choose to shrink discomfort. This can be a physical or an emotional discomfort like anger or sadness. I'll ask you about it next time! Wonderful, give yourselves a hand!

Youth Variation

Teenagers will enjoy the same script as adults. Elementary school children also adore this activity. While not necessary, it is possible to add entertainment after explaining the concept of the mind as a headlight. A facilitator who is comfortable with silliness can do a fun skit about any kind of pain (vaccination, flu, dentist, etc.) by getting a list of what most children do when in pain, invite a volunteer to playfully imitate *him- or herself* in pain, and then demonstrate the usefulness of controlling the secret switch in our mind to reduce pain. When a facilitator is comfortable with this and fully committed, humor and silliness always capture young people's interest and make them more willing to follow the facilitator's instructions for the rest of the project.

Tasting with Mindlight: The Mysterious Fruit Exercise!

Words of wisdom: Our senses often silently provide us with absolutely extraordinary, scrumptious experiences that we fail to notice.

Intention: Increase awareness and mindfulness associated with the daily activity of eating.

Props: A whiteboard or big paper pad, and a marker. A small paper cup or paper towel for each participant and two small pieces (roughly 1 cm × 1 cm) of an uncommon dried fruit such as a sample of natural fruit leather, hibiscus flowers, dragon fruit, or dried melon. Whatever is chosen, it must not look like any identifiable fruit to avoid triggering the mental knowing of what it is ahead of time or, with children, the "I don't like that" issue. The exercise works best when the fruit remains mysterious and can be discovered through sensing only (check your audience for food allergies). For facilitators who enjoy engaging young children with playful skits, it can be fun to use a remote control and a screen of any kind to demonstrate "screen eating," and to pretend eating mindlessly with plastic foods.

Time: 30–45 minutes

Overview
This is a modified version of the brilliant raisin exercise developed by Jon Kabat-Zinn. This exercise redefines people's relationship with the food they eat, and opens a new world of awareness for our taste buds. The exercise was originally modified to suit young audiences who can respond rather negatively to the original exercise ("This is dumb"), express strong dislike for raisins ("I hate raisins!"), criticize the kind of raisins ("I only like the black ones"), or refuse to pay attention to the instruction by talking to their neighbors. It was changed to include some mystery, which always captures people's attention, regardless of their age, and to avoid the automatic dislike.

Figure 5.2. The Life Story of a Fruit.

The mysterious fruit exercise is now quite successful with young people *and* adults. The purpose of choosing an unknown and mysterious fruit is to keep everyone's mind open with curiosity and focused on the sensory experience. If it is necessary to use raisins, you can still claim that it is a fruit most people have never *really tasted* before (everyone typically eats those mindlessly and quickly). Interestingly, when people successfully complete the exercise, the majority of them share with surprise that they thought they hated raisins, but they actually really like them!

Facilitation

Can anyone remind us of what we talked about last time? Did some of you use your mindlight or think about things in a slightly different way? Is anyone willing to share an example?

Today we'll discover something new about the mind. As we now know, the mind can be quite powerful, but it is especially so when it accesses a lot of information. For example, do you make better decisions when you have just a little information or when you have a lot? Our mind gets information from many sources by carefully watching the world around us, and in particular, by connecting to our senses. Can anyone remind us what senses are exactly, and how many we have? (Take responses). *Today we'll train our minds to get a lot of information from one of our senses: taste. Since we are bound to eat all our lives, we may as well do so with awareness and appreciation!*

Children have about 10 million taste buds in their mouth, and older adults have only about half of that. Children are lucky, and can really taste fully their favorite food if they want to … if they're mindful! Adults have fewer taste buds and therefore ought to be paying attention while eating to taste more! Just for fun, let me ask what are some of your favorite foods that you'd like to taste more? When you're eating these foods, you can generally eat them with one of three different attitudes:

1. *Very fast on the run, thinking about the next activity you want to do.*
2. *Moderately fast in front of a screen, watching a movie, YouTube video, or texting.*
3. *Slowly and mindfully.*

What are the effects of eating fast or in front of a screen? Let's list those together (write on a big paper or board if available; this list can be used to contrast with mindful eating later).

When you eat with mindlight, your mind is so focused on what you're eating that it discovers all sorts of details you had never noticed before, AND it can better store that information in your memory. Not only do you enjoy your food more but you also can remember how it tastes later! You can actually remember what chocolate cake tastes like, and feel the saliva in your mouth. Some people can even reexperience the taste! Another advantage is to avoid food poisoning; many animals pay attention to their food and can avoid some food poisoning. Humans can do the same, in some circumstances, if they pay more attention. So using our mindlight when we eat offers several advantages.

Let's do a special exercise to practice this skill. I will invite you into a meditation like last time. After the instructions, I will ask you to close your eyes, to position your feet flat on the floor, and to take a few slow deep breaths... Leave a hand on your lap, ready to receive a small paper cup that looks like this (show). *At first, just hold it in your hand until I've finished distributing cups to everyone, and while you're there, eyes closed, notice the sensations associated with holding a cup! Do not eat the mysterious fruit until I invite you to do so, as there will be specific instructions you'll need to hear for the experiment to be fun. I will also ask you to make some observations and answer some questions, mentally (not aloud), that we'll discuss later. You will be eating two small pieces of a mysterious fruit that most of you have likely never tasted before.*

Okay, let's start! Put your feet flat on the floor, close your eyes, and position your hands in a relaxed way on your thighs. Take very slow deep breaths... Feel your body settling on your chair and becoming more relaxed (silently and slowly distribute the paper cups with the pieces of fruit). *Pay attention to your face. ... Are your eyes heavy and closed,... is your nose breathing well, ... is your jaw relaxed? ... Feel your tongue. As many of you know, the tongue is covered by tiny cells called taste buds. ... Feel the saliva in your mouth; it tells you if you drank enough water today. ... If you're hungry, it's ready to receive food and break it down into smaller pieces so your body can digest it. ... Now that everyone has a paper cup in their hands, open your eyes very slowly, without talking or moving, and simply look in the cup. ... Examine the mysterious fruit with your eyes only; notice its bumps, color, and texture. ... Very slowly, as slowly as you can, allow your fingers to move toward it, and pick it up very gently, as if it could break. Examine it more closely. It may be small, but this mysterious fruit has received sunshine, rain, and wind, and it grew from the rich soil of the earth. It was on a plant that had green leaves. A farmer watched it grow, making sure it had enough water and was ripening well. Feel grateful toward the farmer who took care of your fruit. A worker picked it up with many others, put it in a box, cleaned it, and loaded it on a truck. Feel grateful toward the worker who saw it and picked it up. This tiny mysterious fruit was then driven to a place where someone else unloaded it, packaged it, and placed it on a shelf in a store. Then I came to buy it for you. This small mysterious fruit has a long story attached to it and will soon become part of you (see Figure 5.2 for a visual accompaniment). Smell it very slowly, bring it to your lips slowly, and notice the saliva as your mouth gets ready to receive it. You may now place the mysterious fruit in your mouth, slowly. Do not swallow until I tell you to. Take the time to chew and discover the bursts of sweetness. Notice, if you can, the difference between its inner and outer texture. Watch out for the impulse to swallow too quickly. There are different shapes of taste buds over your tongue. Try to discover where the sugar-tasting cells are—some scientists believe that not all of your tongue can taste sugar and sweetness, only certain areas, and other scientists disagree. Experiment and form your own opinion. Do you feel sweetness on the side of your tongue, on its tip, or in the middle?*

When you're ready and have tasted fully, you may swallow the mysterious fruit. Feel it sliding down the back of your throat and follow its journey to your stomach until you feel it no more. It has become a part of you. Notice that you are one piece of fruit heavier.

Next slowly repeat with the second piece. Look at it slowly with your eyes. You may actually call this mysterious fruit by your name since it'll become you … you can even experience appreciation for it since it will contribute to your growing body and health. Try to notice something you hadn't noticed before—maybe a different shape or color tone or edge. … When you're ready, at your own pace, slowly taste it with joy and curiosity … see if it tastes a little different as every piece is unique. Take the time to feel it … feel the explosion of taste … notice how long it lasts. Does it shift into another taste? Is the skin of the fruit softening? It might start with something a bit hard and become chewy. How fast is the taste changing? I will allow you to notice on your own; try to delay the swallowing over the next minute.

Now that everyone has swallowed pieces of the mysterious fruit, I will count backward from 3 to 1, to end the exercise: 3, you can probably still taste some of the sweetness in your mouth, enjoy; 2, feel your entire body being satisfied; 1, take a deep breath of satisfaction, and open your eyes slowly. When you're ready, raise your hand to share what you've noticed and discovered.

Discussion Questions

- *What was it like? What did you notice? How would you describe the taste? Did you discover a special place on your tongue that tasted sugar?* (Historically it was believed to be the front area of the tongue only, but this is currently debated).
- *What difference does it make to pay attention to what goes into your food (sun, rain …)?*
- *What difference does it make to pay attention to what goes into your body?*
- *What was it like to call the food by your own name? Would it be helpful to remember this when we eat chips and candy?*

Summary

So today you have discovered that you can gain great enjoyment by focusing your mindlight on tasting your food. You have also discovered that everything you eat is connected to a story. Next time, I'll be curious to ask you how you've used your mindlight when eating, and if you've discovered where we taste salt!

Youth Variation

An introduction that mimics how they eat in a fun but respectful way is valuable. You can just ask them to show you how they eat, at their worst. You can even ask the whole group to do so at the same time, for 10 seconds, which triggers excitement and laughter. Then bring the conversation to what is lost when we do that. State that we'll study a new way and remind participants to really pay attention because there will be specific instructions to follow in order to succeed.

Seeing with Mindlight: The Photograph

Words of wisdom: "Our looking is perfected everyday—but we see less and less. ... By [these] labels we recognize everything but no longer see anything."—Frederick Frank

Intention: Invite people to tune their visual attention span.

Props: The headlight and a postcard, calendar photograph, or pleasant painting containing many detailed elements (nothing overly plain and easy) for each participant. Nature scenery appeals to most adults, while scenery including animals or other youth of the same age tends to be attractive to young people. Decide in advance if you are willing to give these images away or wish to collect them at the end of the exercise.

Time: 30 minutes

Overview

After revisiting people's reflections about the previous week's exercise, the facilitator announces the focus of the day, seeing with mindlight. The activity involves taking a mental photograph of an image, enough to see it mentally when we close our eyes. People struggle with this greatly and have to reopen their eyes often to complete their mental image. It makes visible how much is missing from their internal image.

Facilitation

How many of you have eaten slightly differently at least once this past week? Who might have an example to share with us? Did anyone figure out where we taste salt

in our mouth? You are all correct. Historically scientists thought only the sides of the tongue taste salty and sour, and the back tastes mostly bitter, but some people are now saying they taste everything everywhere!

Today we will talk about using your mindlight with your eyes. Our eyes see tons of things. An image is worth a thousand words, yet we often forget what we see because we do not use our mindlight. Remembering what we see can be very helpful. We can recognize faces, memorize an image of a beautiful place, and remember where we've last seen a lost item. You can choose what will fill your mind. What percentage of what you see do you think you register or remember? Take a second to make a wild guess! For example, how would you describe the walls and doors to this building that you saw before entering this room? Do you have a mental image of them? Let's try to recreate that together. What's right outside this door? (If engaged, continue to ask participants to describe a few other parts of the building/room.)

Today we will practice using our mindlight as a camera and take a mental photograph. Choose one image that you like from this stack, and when everyone has one and is seated quietly, we will all study our image in silence for 10 seconds, which is a lot more time than we regularly look at something. Then we will close our eyes and try to recreate it.

Ready? Let's start the 1-minute timer. Go. Study the border of your image … its four corners … what's in the middle … how items connect with one another … colors. … There are 15 seconds left … 5, 4, 3, 2, 1. … Okay, now close your eyes and try to see your image. Recreate it millimeter by millimeter … how many kinds of green or blue did it contain …were there main characters? Try to see the picture as completely as possible as if you were going to be asked to draw it. Your mind can be like a photo album if you train it well.

When you've done the best you can, estimate for yourself how much of the image you can recreate. Most of it? 50%? 25%? After coming up with your estimate, you can open your eyes and look at your photograph again, and give it another try on your own to see if you can enrich and complete your mental image. Count how many times you might need to do this to fully see it in your mind's eye.

Discussion Questions

- *Did you remember more or less of the image than you expected? How many times did you need to recreate the image?*
- *What was hardest to remember? Did you discover any tricks to help you remember?*
- *Had you realized before how little we register of what we see?*

Summary

Today we practiced really seeing. Abilities will vary from person to person because some of us are really good at registering visual information, while others are better with auditory information. What matters is not comparing ourselves to others, but making an effort to stretch our own limits and improve. I encourage you to see more this week, when you walk on the street, even in your own home, or elsewhere, and I'll ask you about new details you've uncovered!

General Variations

Facilitators who really enjoy this activity can add a third practice with easy images and ask people to draw what they noticed without relooking. It can also be as simple as listing the image's items by name in order to avoid triggering a sense of failure for people who do not draw very well (for example: there was one bird, two types of grass, 10 trees, etc.).

Seeing with Mindlight: The Changing Game

Words of wisdom: "We see what we want to see, not what is actually before our eyes. … We may have to tune our seeing just as we tune an instrument, to increase its sensitivity, its range, its clarity."—Jon Kabat-Zinn

Intention: Invite people to realize how much information is lost when we do not pay attention and practice taking control of their visual attention span.

Props: Nothing for participants, but the facilitator should dress with easily modifiable items such as a watch, jewelry, buttoned shirts, a belt, shoelaces, etc. Also, keep in mind that participants need room to stand and move around in this game.

Time: 45 minutes

Overview

After revisiting people's reflections about the previous week's exercise, the facilitator announces the focus of the day, Level 2 of seeing with mindlight. The game "Change Three Things"[1] is explained and demonstrated. In a nutshell, it consists of facing and observing a partner for 10 seconds, turning around (so as to not be seen by the partner) and changing three things about our appearance, then facing the partner again to guess what was changed. Both participants secretly change items at the same time and take turns guessing what was altered. They will repeat this sequence dynamically three times with a different partner, and an unexpected instruction will be given with the fourth and last partner. In this game, time must be monitored carefully to give just enough for people to succeed. The observing segment can take about 10 seconds, but turning around and changing three things can take 10–20 seconds depending on the age group. Facilitators need to watch the group and announce the next step when most people have succeeded in changing three things, before they start waiting. This exercise requires flexibility and creativity, which can be a worthy stretch for many. After participants have observed their fourth partner and turned around, the facilitator asks them to name each other's eye color, which is unexpected. The exercise ends with applauding everyone's effort even though about half of the people will not have noticed their partner's eye color.

Facilitation

Has anyone looked at things a little differently this week based on last week's photograph exercise? (Listen and comment on their observations). *Thanks for sharing!*

We are continuing our practice of using our mindlight to better pay attention to what we see, and will play a game. You're going to pay attention to a partner, look carefully for 8–10 seconds, and then, when I give you the signal, you will turn around and change three things. It can be anything, a zipper, hair position, an elastic band, shoelaces, a button, a watch, a cap turned around, a belt, a ring on another finger, removing a sweater, etc. … After you've changed three things, wait for my signal, and when everyone is ready, I'll ask you to turn around again and try to figure out what your partner has changed. Can I have a volunteer to help me demonstrate? (Demonstrate with volunteer). *Thanks for helping me demonstrate!*

We will do this three times with different people. When I say switch, you quickly take a new partner, whoever is available and right beside you. Your partner doesn't need to be someone you know or like. Don't look for a friend because you will not have enough time; this game moves very quickly. Let's try it. Okay, stand up with the person on your right and find a place to stand 2 feet apart and start noticing each other. I will only give a few seconds for the noticing. NOTICE … TURN AROUND … CHANGE THREE THINGS …TURN AROUND … TAKE TURNS GUESSING THE DIFFERENCES … SWITCH PARTNERS (repeat instructions dynamically three more times). … *Try to find some new things to change every time, if you can. I know it can be challenging, but try. You'll be surprised to find out that there is more than you think.*

Observe your fourth and last partner carefully, as there will be a trick question. Okay, turn around. Is everyone turning their back to their partner? Okay, what was the color of your partner's eyes? Think about it for a second, close your eyes, and silently search your mind (give 10 seconds). *Now you can look at your partner. Give yourselves a hand and go back to your seat!*

Discussion Questions

- *How was it? Was it hard to change three things? What is easy to notice about people? Did your mind get into certain habits such as noticing buttons and shoelaces?*
- *What does this say about the mindlight? How can we keep it noticing as much as possible instead of getting into habits?*
- *How did your mindlight feel when it was on? The mind has to be flexible. Were you surprised to discover all the things you can change? Raise your hand if you were surprised.*

Summary

Today we discovered the need to practice using our mindlight for truly seeing. Think about the words of wisdom by Jon Kabat-Zinn (see earlier in this exercise), *and I'll ask how you have looked at certain things differently next week.*

Youth Variation

During the demonstration, it is wise to request that the group does not help you guess the volunteer's changes. Young people really like this game and want to talk to each other afterward. It's fine to give them 2–3 minutes to do so before bringing everyone back to a big group discussion.

Touching with Mindlight: The Unusual Bump

Words of wisdom: Since we live on Earth and in air, there is *always* something that touches us.

Intention: Practice paying attention to tactile information.

Props: Bumpy small objects, one or two per participant, such as pebbles, seashells, interesting erasers, keys, small wooden toys, etc. ... These objects can all be different as long as they're not obvious to guess right away (like a spoon). People will also need to hold a small, blank flashcard or a piece of paper (big enough to draw the object), a pencil, and sit on chairs.

Time: 20–30 minutes

Overview

Participants are asked to stand up silently, eyes closed, and a small object is placed on their chair so that when they sit, their mid-thigh will be over it. If anyone has physical injuries or back problems, they can lie down on the floor and the object can be placed on their belly. Participants are invited to first notice the sensations, then make mental observations and guesses about what they are sitting on. After about 1 minute, they are asked to draw the shape of the object(s) on a flashcard, based on their sensations. This last part is rather challenging and increases people's focus on the sensations. Most people, old and young, do not get an exact representation and that is to be expected—the purpose is mainly to notice tactile sensations. People are then asked to take the object in their hands *without opening their eyes*. This must be emphasized many times by reminding them it will be more fun and special to feel something with their eyes closed. At this point, participants can usually guess what the object is.

Facilitation

Who remembers what we talked about last time? Can anyone share some stories of seeing certain things or even people differently?

Today we're going to talk about the sense of touch. Our skin can feel incredible things, give us important information, and relay wonderful sensations. For example, the sense of touch allows you to feel the softness of your pet's fur, or if something is swollen after an accident. Think about it; we're always touching something! Clothes, the ground, air, etc. … Paying attention to these sensations can help you avoid blisters in your shoes if you're aware of what your skin is "telling you." There are 100 sensor cells for every 2 mm at the tips of our fingers. Isn't that incredible? Look at a finger and imagine 100 little dots waiting to tell you about what you'll be touching!

Today we will try an exercise similar to the story of the Princess and the Pea. Does everyone know this traditional story? Who can summarize it for us? (Summary is shared). *Do you think she was using her mindlight? Here's what we'll do: we'll start by holding a pencil and a small piece of paper in our hands and standing up. We'll do a very short version of a standing meditation. During that time I will place a mysterious object on your chair. When I tell you so, without looking, very slowly, you will sit down and try to pay attention to what you feel about the object under you. Eventually you will try to draw it on your paper. This entire exercise has to be done silently so that you can all concentrate. If someone sneezes or makes noise, just ignore them and keep your mindlight focused on your own experience.*

Okay, let's start: stand up ... close your eyes ... and focus on your breath while I place objects on everyone's chair. Feel the air going in and out of your lungs, slowly. Quickly scan what it's like to stand up, how your feet are feeling ... legs ... knees ... abdomen ... arms ... neck ... and head. Be grateful to your feet and legs, they are holding your body upright all day long. Feel the air go all the way from your nose down to your toes.

(When an object has been placed on every chair) *Now you can very slowly sit down on your chair. You'll notice an object is there; do not touch it with your hands. Find a way of settling on the object so as to feel it without being too bothered by it, again, without using your hands and while remaining silent. Try to feel its shape ... its thickness ... if it's soft or hard ... see if you can feel the edges. Pay attention to these tactile sensations, to what your skin is telling you. Keep on breathing slowly.. When you're ready, try to draw its shape based on your mind's observations. You don't have to guess what it is; you can simply draw sensations, bumps, or edges. We are often more skilled at sensing with our eyes closed, so you can peek at your paper, but mostly try to keep your eyes closed.*

Now that everyone has attempted to draw the object, still keeping your eyes closed slowly reach for the object and remove it from under your leg, without peeking. I repeat, without opening your eyes, try to just feel the object in your hands, and maybe guess what it is. Still without opening your eyes, feel all its edges, textures, and temperature, and notice whether it feels the same way everywhere. Different places in your hand will likely feel different aspects of it. I will count from 5 to 1 and you will then open your eyes and look at your mysterious object. 5, 4, 3, 2, 1.

Discussion Questions

- *What did you notice when you were sitting on the object? Was it hard to feel its edges? What did you feel?*
- *When you took it in your hands, what was different about feeling the object with your eyes closed?*
- *How would it be to really feel things we hold in our hands every day? Could that be helpful sometimes?*

Summary

Today we practiced sensing tactile information. This week, try to notice a few things you regularly touch without having paid much attention to them before. I will ask you to share some examples next week! Give yourself a hand!

Youth Variation

For facilitators who like playfulness with children, a student volunteer can be chosen to act an improvised story of "The Student and the Bump," which is essentially a parody of "The Princess and the Pea." The purpose of the skit is to provide some fun, concrete, and visual demonstration of these ideas. Children may be tempted to peek—this can be prevented by asking, "Will it be more or less fun if you peek?" At the very end of the exercise, when instructed to open their eyes, children can be given a few minutes of excited conversation with their friends before the big group discussion. On a separate day, another fun variation is to invite students to silently sit near each other in rows of chairs, close their eyes (or wear blindfolds), and circulate special objects such as fur, an uncooked noodle, a sand bowl, etc. ... and just feel without needing to identify the object or label out loud what they are sensing.

Mindlight and Sound: Discovering the Sound of Silence

Words of wisdom: For most people, a moment of inner silence is like a shooting star: you have to search for it, catch it, and marvel with awe while you see it, as it usually doesn't last very long.

Intention: Listen to, and be comfortable with, silence.

Time: 20 minutes

Props: A chime or meditation bell. Adults only: earplugs for each participant. Children and teens are usually not comfortable putting on earplugs, so they can just plug their ears with their hands.

Overview

Participants are invited to listen to silence with and without their ears plugged for 1–3 minutes depending on their age and experience (on average: children 1 minute, teens 2 minutes, and adults 3 minutes).

Facilitation

We rarely stop to pay attention to silence, partly because we don't perceive silence as interesting to study, but mostly because there is rarely silence outside AND inside of us! How many of you can stop your mind from thinking? Can you put it on pause when you want to? Thinking is a tool, and most of us have lost control over it and can't stop. For most people, a moment of silence is like a shooting star or if we are lucky, a meteor shower: you have to search for it, catch it, and marvel with awe while you see it, as it usually doesn't last very long! We'll experiment briefly with listening to moments of silence inside and outside of us, and divide the exercise into two parts. First, to help us better pay attention, we will change our habitual way of hearing and reduce some of the external noise, either with earplugs or with our hands.

With your ears plugged, you can hear more sounds from inside your body. For example, try to discern the sounds of your inhale and exhale, your heartbeat, your pulse. ...What is it like to be inside of yourself sound-wise? Notice the silence after you breathe out, avoid thinking if you can, and try just marveling at the near silence. When your mind wanders, gently bring it back to observing silence. Try to catch your internal silence and if there is external noise, leave that outside of you, don't react to it; the reaction is what brings sound "inside" of you. We will spy "on" silence for 1–3 minutes, and when I ring the chime, we'll unplug our ears and shift to the second part of the exercise, which is to just listen to external sounds. In this second part, try to just be an observer, and stop your mind from thinking. If necessary, count how many different sounds you hear in order to keep your mind anchored in the present moment for 1 to 3 minutes! The intention in both parts of the exercise is just to catch moments of inner and outer silence, so I will not speak. Let us all take a deep breath, close our eyes, cover our ears, and begin.

Discussion Questions

- *Did you catch any moment of silence? How was it? What was special about it?*
- *How was it to contrast with hearing sounds afterward? How many sounds did you count? Let's list them together.*

Summary

A famous author, Thich Nhat Hanh, says that "silence is a powerful sound." Think about that this week and see if you can discover valuable aspects of silence.

Youth Variation

No variations necessary, aside from children using their hands to cover their ears instead of earplugs.

Mind over Sounds: An Unusual Orchestra

Words of wisdom: The silent mind hears delicious sounds.

Intention: This exercise has three goals: 1) help people realize that they have some control over the sounds, noises, and words they hear; 2) reduce the constant chatter of thinking; and 3) have a fun, creative sound experience.

Props: Two sets of recordings of different sounds. Examples of these include birdsong collections, bug noises, ocean sounds, etc. With children, you could have one or two sound-making Audubon stuffed birds—this is not necessary, but it is fun. Everyone must sit as a tight group in two or three rows of chairs in order to create an "orchestra."

Time: 40–50 minutes (or can easily be divided in two or more sessions)

Overview

After reviewing the previous week's applications, the facilitator explains the importance of being aware of our mindlight's attention to sounds. Two simple exercises can be facilitated.

The first involves consciously keeping the mind's focus on solving a problem while a distracting sound is deliberately and playfully introduced in the group. The group is encouraged to modify their experience of the unpleasant sound distraction and develop strategies to sustain their concentration.

The second activity focuses on remembering what is heard, and highlights how many of us remember very few bird sounds because we just don't pay attention, even though we hear so many (see Figure 5.3). After listening to a recording, participants are invited to form an orchestra. The group is divided into two teams, each assigned to listen intently for 1–2 minutes (at the most) to bird songs or ocean waves recordings. People choose a sound to remember and then playfully repeat a version of the chosen sound, as if performing in an orchestra. For this last exercise, the facilitator needs to be fully committed to the role of orchestra director. Without the proper playful scaffolding of the exercise, people will not feel comfortable making any sounds. They need to trust that everyone is on board. This is usually accomplished by moving

Figure 5.3. Birds Have Fantastic Songs That Our Mind Often Tunes Out.

swiftly from one small step to another, first asking them to pretend they are performers and to stand as professionals; second, asking them all together to make a simple warm-up sound such as "aaaaa," which can be modulated for about 5–20 seconds by the facilitator like an orchestra director gesturing them to increase or decrease the volume. Hearing everyone contributing to this simple task is generally enough for participants to feel more confident and to fully embrace the command to mimic their chosen bird or wave sound, all at once, as an orchestra. Ending with the agreed-upon gesture for stopping, and a dynamic "give yourselves a hand," leaves people with a fun, energizing, and memorable experience of how to listen, pay attention, and remember oral information.

Facilitation

Who can remind us what we talked about last time? Has anyone tried using these ideas? Today we will continue our exploration of listening. Sounds are one more tool your mindlight can use to help you in many situations.

We are surrounded by sounds, some we like and some we don't. As we've discussed before, our mind is like a light: it can be constantly moving around in a scattered way, it can take in great perspectives, or it can be still and have an intense focus on details. It's important to realize that we can control what our mind does with what happens around us. For example, what we hear and listen to, and what we remember.

If you wish to concentrate on a test or task, your mind can actually transform or block out other sounds in order to help you accomplish what you want. For example, you can mentally transform the sound of a highway into an imaginary waterfall! It also means that if you don't control your mindlight and start repeatedly thinking, for example, "This clock's sound is so annoying," this thought may lead to missing out on precious moments or important information like these instructions, without even realizing it.

In other words, our mind can control what we do with sounds, whether they are pleasant or not. Sometimes we find a sound satisfying, yet we don't even listen to it (like ocean sounds) and other times we immerse ourselves fully in sounds like our favorite music. Similarly, with unpleasant sounds: we can get really annoyed by the sound of someone else, but later ignore the background sound of a radio … raise a finger if you've noticed that! Isn't it strange that our mind does that? Let's try to practice having more control over our mind with fun exercises.

Level 1: *Blocking Distracting Sounds*

Who can give me two or three big numbers to add up? (Make the complexity age appropriate). *Now I will play a distracting audio recording from my iPhone every few seconds, while we all try to add up these numbers* (give 1 minute).

Done. Did we succeed? Yes, we could concentrate in spite of the sounds, because we focused our minds on the math problem. We can put certain tasks in the forefront of our mind with our mindlight and give them attention, and we can put sounds in the background. We know sounds are there but we don't react to them or give them any feelings or attention. This is the trick: if someone makes noises and we get upset and start thinking, it's the upset feelings focusing on the sound that get in our way, not the sound itself. You would probably not even hear the sound if you were reading your favorite book and in the middle of its suspense. How many of you were able to focus on the math problem in spite of the iPhone recording? Were you able to ignore it or put it in the back of your mind? Did any of you transform the sound into something else? Great! Your attention, your mindlight, is like a remote control for your brain. You can practice your power to switch the channels as you wish.

Level 2: Remembering Sounds

My second point has to do with choosing to remember what we hear. Essentially, we're more likely to remember what we pay attention to. For example, how many types of bird sounds might you have heard before in your life? Who thinks more than five different sounds? 10? 20? 30? Most big cities across the world host more than 2,000 different species of birds! How many of you can recreate the song of four or five birds just now? No one! What happened? You probably haven't used your mindlight and paid attention, because no one taught you how to use it. Your ears can detect up to 20,000 different vibrations, and you get to choose which ones you wish to remember. Today we will practice using the power of your mind to choose to remember what you hear.

Let's practice how we remember what we pay attention to. Most of the time, in order to remember something, our brain needs to be active and "do" something with the material, like wondering about a question, feeling an emotion associated with it, or connecting it to other memories already stored in our brains. We're going to do a fun experiment to practice this skill, using sounds. I'd like to divide you into two groups. One group will listen to an audio recording on this side of the room, and pay attention to this recording only. The other group will listen to another recording playing completely different sounds. There's no need to move; just notice which sound you are supposed to listen to, and listen very intently as there will be a test afterward. I will ask you to first close your eyes and take a few deep breaths. Settle in your chair comfortably. Let's make sure everyone is silent, relaxed, and ready to listen to the sounds. Please keep your comments to yourself, and do not make any noise so it doesn't affect everyone's concentration. Okay, let's start and listen intently ... mirror the sound mentally, with your whole mind. The secret in doing this is to repeat the sound in your mind many times, silently. Now here's the most important instruction: I'm going to ask you to listen to the recording and choose one sound that you will have to repeat after I end the recording. Make sure you listen well enough to repeat it afterward. You will only have 2 minutes to listen and notice a sound well enough to repeat it. When I pause the recording, I will ask you to be silent until everyone gets to repeat their sound out loud in a special way. Ready? Close your eyes and here we go (two different recordings are started at the same time and played for 1 or 2 minutes).

Keep repeating the memory of your chosen sound in your mind, and pretend that you are world-famous performers all dressed up professionally. You are just about to start a show in front of thousands of people. You must stand straight, look elegant, fix your hair, and feel competent. I am your orchestra director. With my hand I will gesture like this, to increase your volume, reduce it, or stop (show the hand motions). *We will do a 1-minute warmup of our voices: on the count of three, everyone says "aaaaaaaaaaa." 1, 2, 3 ... and stop! Great! Now we are ready for our show. Everyone will sing the sound you have memorized over and over again until I gesture to stop. You have to all stop at exactly the same time. Okay, and a 1, and a 2, and a 1, 2, 3!* (Direct as an orchestra director would, take yourself seriously, alternate between having the two different groups louder or softer, and finish with a grand final crescendo and then stop firmly after a few seconds. Invite people to give themselves a good hand of applause and bow!)

Discussion Questions

- *What was it like to listen intently to sounds? What was it like to listen with your eyes closed?*
- *What did you do in your mind to remember the sound? What was it like to repeat the sound in your mind? Was your mind able to stay focused on the recording of the sound?*
- *Were you surprised you could make these sounds?*

Summary

You can choose what you listen to, how you listen to it, the effect it has on your mind, and what you remember.

Youth Variation

None necessary; elementary school children absolutely adore this exercise. With adolescents, this can only be facilitated if the teens are comfortable with improvisation and their fellow group members. While these games may not, in isolation, train young people to pay attention to instructions, they increase their understanding of the process and give them an experience of, and a method for, grabbing their attention and using it on a desired task.

An optional fun follow-up to the second exercise is the bingo game "Audio Safari," where people listen to animal sounds and guess which animals they correspond to on bingo cards. The game is harder than expected, as few people really pay attention to the sounds of animals in isolation (i.e., without the visual clue).

Smelling with Mindlight: Curious Smells

Words of wisdom: Many moments are perfumed with exquisite scents we often fail to notice.

Intention: Discover the sense of olfaction and use it to improve memory.

Props: Three to five fresh and very fragrant flowers such as Stargazer lilies, roses, Miletonia orchids, etc., and a cooler in which to store the flowers and hide their fragrance. Alternatively, essential oils or food extracts can be used and must be clearly identifiable by the participants such as lavender, mint, coconut, or almond extract. It is best to avoid sugary smells.

Time: 20 minutes

Overview

Provide a silent, closed-eye context where participants focus solely on smelling various natural fragrances that they can later practice recognizing.

Facilitation

Has anyone noticed interesting sounds in the past week? Any sounds you made an effort to remember? Which sense is left to explore? That's right, the sense of smell.

Humans' sense of smell is less developed than that of other creatures such as sharks, which smell blood miles away, or dogs, which can detect 100 more smells than we can (they have about 500 million smell cells while we only have about 50 million!). Even so, most people can tell apart up to 10,000 different smells because of the carpet-like bundle of smell cells in our upper nose! Smells are processed in the same part of the brain that handles feelings, so sometimes a smell might trigger a memory or an emotion, without us even realizing it. Our sense of smell can protect us from eating food that has turned bad, can help us remember where we put something, and can even help us with pain. Most of the time, however, we don't pay attention to smells. Today we're going to practice using this sense as this is our last session before your pain test next week! I am now confident that you are all fully equipped with lots of strategies to handle pain very well.

In a minute, we will start by closing our eyes and focusing on our breath. Then, when everyone is peaceful and calm, I will take out some mysterious things that have a pleasant fragrance from this cooler and move them around in the group. They will be numbered item 1, 2, 3, 4, and 5. It is more fun if you don't open your eyes and just focus on the fragrance. This is a very unique chance to smell something without seeing it, or trying to imagine what it looks like! At the end, I will tell you to open your eyes and you will be able to see the items.

So let's start. Place your feet flat on the floor and take a deep breath, slowly. … Feel the air flowing up into your nose, down your throat, and into your belly. Take another slow, silent, deep breath and focus on the air moving in your nose. Notice the sensations inside your nasal cavity, whether you can feel the air everywhere or only in certain areas. See if you can feel the tiny little hairs dancing under each in-breath. If at any point you find your mind wandering, gently return it to your sense of smell. Now I will take item 1 out from my cooler and move it slowly in front of each person. Keep your eyes closed and try to notice the faint impression of scent when I am far from you, and the stronger fragrance when I am closer. How long can you smell it? … Now I am taking out fragrant item 2. Smell the scent with great curiosity and enjoy. Notice where in your nose you might pick up the scent. Only a small area in our nose has cells that can detect smells. … Now I am taking out fragrant item 3. Fill your body with the scented air. Try to smell in the same way you would eat a delicious fruit or dessert. Dwell on the sensation, savor it, and enjoy it, as if you were eating a wonderful fragrant treat. … Now I am taking out fragrant item 4. Smell as if you were a young child smelling this for the first time and being curious about the scent! … Now I am taking out fragrant item 5, our last one. Notice any image that may come to your mind about this fragrance, or any ideas about this object's color. … Keep on breathing deeply and relaxing with this wonderful fragrance. The fragrances are filling up the room, and you can relax and enjoy. Notice how quickly we become accustomed to smells and how easily we can forget about them. Our body habituates to certain sensations and we often don't notice them after a while. If you can still smell the fragrance, try to imagine what the object will look like. I will count backward from 5 to 1, and when I reach 1, you will slowly end the exercise. 5, take a deep, relaxing breath; … 4, feel how relaxed your body is; … 3, enjoy the peace inside of you; … 2; … and 1, open your eyes and admire the beautiful flowers!

Discussion Questions

- *What was it like to focus on the scents entering your nose? Were you able to notice when I moved the flowers closer and further away from you?*
- *Was anyone able to feel as if they were eating the smell? What difference does it make if we learn to really smell with our mindlight?*
- *Does paying attention to scents affect how we breathe? Can this be helpful sometimes when we're sad or hurt?*

Summary
We have to wrap up. Today we learned how to use our mindlight to notice and enjoy scents in the same way we eat delicious foods. This will be one of your many strategies when I bring the pain test next week! In the meantime, you can all practice using your senses to take control of your minds and contribute to shaping every day into a great day!

Note
As discussed in Chapter 2, one or two participants may say that they can't breathe through their nose. If this occurs, the facilitator can tell them to breathe whichever way they can, which ideally can be a combination of nose and mouth, and pretend that they're breathing mostly through their nose. They can focus on the small amount of air that does go through as opposed to the blockage. People who succeed at focusing on the small amount of air that does get through their nasal cavity often report breathing better afterward and feeling less congested.

Participants often have a shiver of excitement and nervousness when the mysterious pain test is mentioned. Reassure them that it is not *very* painful, and that they are in control of whether they do it or not, and for how long. The actual painful element is kept entirely secret until the very last minute.

The Pain Test: Level 1

Words of wisdom: We are blessed with little power over the outside and immense power over our inside.

Intention: Provide a structured environment where people can test their newly acquired strategies and develop a greater confidence in their abilities to handle hardship, both physical and emotional.

Props: A cooler with two cubes of ice per participant and five extra for those who might need replacements. These cubes need to be big (roughly 2" × 3"), otherwise they melt very quickly in some people's hands. You will also need a small paper cup for each person to hold their ice cubes and collect the dripping water from the melting ice. Optional: bring another bouquet of flowers, in its own secret container, to discreetly pull out during the pain test, without telling people about it ahead of time.

Time: 30–45 minutes

Overview

Depending on the age group, the facilitator may choose to present some research on pain management in the introduction. There are many fascinating accounts! For example, as mentioned in Chapter 1, *some mindfulness masters control their minds to such an extent that they feel no pain at all, even when experimenters shine a painful laser light on their hands. A number of fMRI studies have scientifically confirmed these claims by measuring levels of activation of certain structures in these masters' brains* (Smalley & Winston, 2010).

After a thorough review of previous exercises and pain management strategies, the facilitator asks participants to guess what the pain test might be. This is usually a lot of fun! People come up with very creative ways of assessing pain tolerance!

Invariably, a participant will guess correctly that the pain test is holding ice. Holding ice is a perfect pain test. Doing so for a second may be easy, but holding it for 3–4 minutes can feel uncomfortable and provide a nice challenge. Giving too much time runs the risk of the ice being completely melted long before the end of the exercise. The facilitator may choose to silently walk around the room and add a piece of hard ice in the cup of people whose overly warm hands melt theirs too quickly. In both of the following tests make sure to end the practice before participants lose their excitement and pride in their success.

Facilitation

This is the big day when we get to use all the strategies discussed in our sessions! Let's start by reviewing all of our senses and how we can use them to deal with pain and struggles. Who remembers which sense we talked about last week? Has anyone used or noticed scents this week? Thanks for the great example. What are the other senses we can use when we're in pain? Can you give me an example of what you can do with each of these senses when you're facing a hardship?

I am confident that you are now ready to do your pain test! Can anyone guess what it is? (Smile).

It is ice! Ice is easy to handle for a short amount of time, but if we hold it longer, it quickly becomes uncomfortable. Today we will hold ice for 4 minutes! I will first ask you to sit quietly with your eyes closed, focusing on your breath and relaxing your body, while I distribute cups of ice. Wait until I give you the signal to pick up your first cube as we will start all together, then you'll have 2 minutes to handle the sensations on your own without me talking. You may wish to keep your cup under your cube to catch the melted water. If your cube melts, you can pick up the next one in your cup as long as you move slowly and silently. If your ice melts too quickly and you run out, you can silently raise your other hand and I will add another piece in your cup, one time only. When there is no more ice, just focus on the water sensation in your hands.

Okay, let's start (facilitator distributes cups while talking). *Pain triggers three systems in the brain that all contribute to the experience of suffering—senses, feelings, and thoughts—and you have control over these! That's why a common adage says that pain is unavoidable but suffering is optional! With practice, everyone has the capacity to limit and subdue a very significant amount of pain. Place your feet flat on the floor, close your eyes, place your hands on your lap, and take a deep, slow, silent breath. Feel the air going in and out of your body ... allow it to go all the way to your feet ... allow it to go all the way to your fingers. Notice the sensation in your hand ... is it warm ... cold ... humid? Find the warmest spot in your hand and feel its radiating sun-like heat. Is the air around us warmer or colder than your hand? Continue to breathe slowly and feel your body become strong and calm like a tree.*

Now that you all have a cup in your hands, take a moment to feel the sensations associated with holding it. Be aware that the ice is on the inside of this cup, and you can already sense its cool temperature. ... You may now pick up your first piece of ice. ... Position the cup right underneath the holding hand to collect any melting water. Pay attention to the coldness of the ice against the warmness of your hand. You can imagine the cold staying outside of your hand as if it was on the other side of a window. See how long you can hold the sensation of warmth in your hand. Focus on what you appreciate, the warmth of your hand, not on what is uncomfortable. When you find the cold to become uncomfortable, shift your focus to your other senses. Which sense would you like to focus on? What comes naturally to your mind? Would you like to notice sounds like the peaceful ticking of a clock? Or the subtle sounds associated with the presence of people around you? Or the sensation of the chair beneath you? You could also notice the sensations in your feet, which are very far from your hands and offer lots of items to observe such as each toe, socks, shoes, floor, etc. ... Sometimes focusing on an area of the body far from the pain works wonderfully well. You can revisit how things are going in your hand and make a decision whether you want to continue the challenge of holding the ice. It's up to you how long you test yourself; just remain still and quiet when you choose to stop. I will now stop talking and allow you to practice your own tricks to handle the discomfort. Remember that focusing on your breath can always help you; it's always there no matter what, and it can anchor you in a calm and peaceful rhythm.

(Allow 2–3 minutes of silence depending on the speed of ice melting that day and people's performance).

Time is up and we will end the exercise slowly. Still in silence, place any remaining ice cubes in your cup, and notice the temperature difference between the ice itself and the water dripping from your fingers. I will now count backward from 3 to 1; focus on some last slow, deep breaths. 3, 2, 1. You can now open your eyes! Congratulations! You have successfully completed 4 minutes of mastery over pain!

Discussion Questions

- *What was it like to handle the discomfort of the cold ice? Which strategies did you use? Let's list them on the board.*
- *How else did you handle the pain? How many of you transformed the sensations into something else? How many of you focused on sounds? Smells? Other sensations in your body?*
- *When was the discomfort or pain at its worst? What was your best moment of controlling the discomfort?*
- *You have all passed the test! Does that leave you feeling different about your abilities? What might you remember about this exercise? What might you do differently now when you get hurt? Can these strategies also apply to when we have sadness or anger?*

Summary

Thanks for sharing your strategies with me and showing me your powerful minds! Remember: you can't control what happens to you, but you can control your internal experiences. Give yourselves a hand!

The Pain Test: Level 2

Words of wisdom: Your body is so much taller, deeper, and greater than a few inches of pain. Choose wisely where your mind dwells.

Intention: Provide a structured environment where people can test again their newly acquired strategies and develop greater confidence. The intent is to reinforce the idea that pain is unavoidable but suffering is optional.

Props: Cut an "acumat" into pieces slightly longer and larger than your participants' feet, or calves (if they choose to lie down). Ideally prepare one piece for each participant, unless you plan to divide the group in two and invite people to take turns.

Time: 30–40 minutes

Overview

Explain that participants will expand their mastery of pain with an unusual prop called an *acumat*, which is covered with about 8,000 acupuncture-like spikes and provides an opportunity to engage in a *fakir*-like experiment. This relatively new device is very uncomfortable at first, but becomes extremely relaxing within 20–40 minutes. As time passes, muscles even generate a little warmth as they deeply relax. The exercise can be kept short since the intention is to practice the discomfort in the early stages of touching an acumat.

Facilitation

The skin has three different types of cells that detect pain and send various signals and information to the brain (Smalley & Winston, 2010). *The skin is our first line of defense against injury, so it's very sensitive and provides great opportunities to practice not reacting to discomfort. Today, we will increase the pain challenge by introducing something that looks very scary and uncomfortable but is actually a fantastic physical therapy and sleep-enhancing device! It is just uncomfortable for a few minutes, which provides a great opportunity to keep your mind open and practice some of the skills we have discussed.*

Lie down on a yoga mat, on the floor, and place your piece of acumat under muscles you'd like to relax or under an area that feels ideal to test your discomfort management skills. You can choose one of your calves (propped on a pillow), an area of your back, a hand (with a book on top for added weight), *or the back of your head. Alternatively, you can place the acumat under your bare feet if you prefer to sit in a chair. The acumat has to be directly on the skin and will trigger no sensation whatsoever on the other side of a t-shirt. Settle down in your chosen position, feel the plastic spikes igniting a signal of recoiling in your skin, and take a deep, slow, silent breath. Feel the air going in and out of your body … allow it to go all the way to the spikes … allow your muscles to relax. In fact, instruct them to let go of tension, and trust that this will be a good experience. If needed, go back and forth between focusing on the sensations of the spikes and focusing on another part of your body. Since this will not last long, I will now let you practice your own strategies for a few minutes. Remember that focusing on your breath can always help you; it's always there no matter what, and can anchor you in a calm and peaceful rhythm. Don't forget to observe, be curious, detached, and let go, as if your body was a doll you were looking at from an observer's point of view.* (Allow 5–10 minutes of silence depending on the age group).

Time is up and we will end the exercise slowly. I will now count backward from 3 to 1; focus on the extent to which the muscles touching the mat have changed. 3, 2, 1. You can now open your eyes! Congratulations!

Discussion Questions

- *What was it like to handle discomfort? Which strategies did you use? Let's list them on the board.*
- *How else did you handle the sensations? How many of you transformed the sensation into something else?*

- *Did you notice a progressive change in the sensations? The mat remained the same; it's your muscles and the relationship to the mat that changed.*
- *What might you remember about this exercise?*

Summary

Remember, research shows that people who choose their focus, and enter the state of mindfulness, tend to suffer much less. They have the skills to dissolve pain, and feel less discomfort when compared to people who simply try to ignore pain. Congratulations, you have all developed an ability to better focus your mind and manage pain! Give yourself a hand!

Youth Variation

This exercise is harder to facilitate with young children who may get overly excited, talkative, and ticklish—it may be simpler to stick with the ice cube challenge.

Note

1. This game was initially developed by Sue Walden of ImprovWorks, San Francisco. For other examples of such games, see Beaudoin and Walden (1997), in *Working with Groups to Enhance Relationships*.

CHAPTER SIX

Fascinating Body Parts

Connecting with the body is an essential aspect of mindfulness meditation. Our bodies and minds are interrelated in all experiences (van der Kolk, 2014), making the mind–body connection an essential component of relaxation and healing. Unfortunately, in a busy world, people tend to become disconnected from their body and are much more focused on their mental experience. The exercises within this chapter are designed to focus on one body part at a time. The intention is to facilitate the mind–body connection in a more structured and specific way. Each exercise begins with fascinating facts about a select body part in order to pique the interest of participants, trigger curiosity, and instill appreciation for the body. The mindfulness inductions that follow these fascinating introductions are about sensing, observing, and connecting to the body rather than thinking.

A Living Balloon Fair

Words of wisdom: Air is within and between us as a binding agent that connects us all into one big substance around the surface of the Earth.

Intention: Increase awareness of our lungs and their ability to take in air.

Time: 20–30 minutes

Props: Bring an empty plastic container such as a gallon to give participants a concrete visual appreciation of the amount of air our lungs breathe. Images of balloon creatures can be helpful with young children or even adults.

Overview
Participants are educated about the lungs and their incredible feats. Induction into a mindfulness state follows with the focus on sensing air inflate the lungs and then imagining that they are transformed into a person balloon (see Figure 6.1), progressively inflating their body. The exercise ends with an awareness of all the other people balloons around them and how they are breathing the same air. The same substance connects us all.

Facilitation
Today we will talk about the fascinating abilities of our lungs. Our lungs are right behind our thoracic cage, well protected with the heart. They look like two balloons, one on each side. Can you guess how many of these containers of air our lungs breathe per minute? (Facilitator listens to participants' guesses). *We breathe 13 pints of air every minute (11,000 liters/day)! This pink organ is very spongy because it is made with about 300 million little balloon-like cells (alveoli) that contain air. It would even float on water if you were to drop a set of lungs full of air in a pool! No other part of the human body would float. Lungs also have something in common with tennis courts, can anyone guess what that is?* (Facilitator listens to participants' guesses). *That's right, it's their size! If we were to smooth all that tissue flat, it would be the size of a tennis court! The lungs can take in a lot of air, but many people don't use them effectively. It is believed that most people, even athletes, use only 25–50% of the oxygen they breathe in because they don't use their diaphragm well. Now who do you think breathes the fastest: dogs, cats, men, women, boys, or girls?* (Listen to participants' guesses). *You are right, it's a dog!*

Figure 6.1. An Inflated Person Balloon.

They take 24 breaths a minute when resting. Many creatures have interesting breathing systems: birds have little tubes and air sacs everywhere in their bodies; amphibians can breathe through their skins; marine mammals like whales and orcas can store large amounts of oxygen in their blood and muscles! Breathing in sends oxygen everywhere in our body, in all our cells! In fact, what you breathe in can get to your brain in 7 seconds (Castro, 2014; Ribeiro, 2017).

Let's find a comfortable position, seated or standing. If you are seated, make sure to sit straight. If you are standing, make sure to bend your knees slightly, keep your shoulders pulled back, your ears above your shoulders, and your feet about shoulder width apart. Relax, minimize the amount of energy you direct at remaining straight and still. … Start by taking in deep breaths and feeling the air flow through your nose, in the back of your throat, and down the tube of the esophagus, which is like a long slide downward to your lungs. … Imagine that these air molecules are happily bumping upon each other as they're making their way down into your lungs. … As you continue to take in more deep breaths, try to feel the amount of air that enters your body (volume). Notice where you feel the greatest amount of air. Is it by your nostrils, inside your nose, sinuses, back of the throat, or mouth? Notice that the floor of your nose is the roof of your mouth! In fact, the roof of your mouth can feel sandwiched between the flow of air entering the nose and then pooling briefly in your mouth before going down your throat. … Notice where your tongue rests when you are relaxing. Is it behind your lower teeth or your upper teeth? Is the air filling up the space above, under, or all around your tongue? Now bring your attention to the air gliding down your throat and filling your lungs. … Can you feel that one is smaller than the other? One has two subsections and the other three. … Try to notice which side is smaller. Inflate your lung balloons to almost their fullest extent, but don't strain. If your lung balloons were a color today, which color might that be? Notice which color comes to your mind as you continue to inflate them fully. … Now on your next inhale, imagine that you discovered your body is actually a person balloon! You can actually inhale deeply and send air all the way down to your legs and inflate your feet! Feel yourself inhaling deeply, sending air down one leg at a time, and inflating carefully every toe, one after the other. … You want to make sure each toe is fully inflated in the first foot. … Make sure you feel each toe expanding with air. … Some toes may be a little harder to feel than others, but they are all important. … Then fill your ankle, calf, knee, and thigh. … Your leg is a nice container of air. … Then switch to the other leg and foot. … Take a deep breath and send air all the way down to the foot of your second leg. … Again, very carefully inflate each toe, one by one, making sure none are neglected or forgotten. … Your person balloon now has two wonderful legs well inflated, as well as the abdomen, which holds the lungs. … You can now inflate your arms, one at a time. … Choose one arm and send air all the way to your fingers. … Feel your arm filling up with fresh air and expanding under your careful attention. … Fill each finger, one by one, with this nourishing oxygen, making sure air makes its way in every corner, under each nail, and inside every fold of skin. … Person balloons usually have wide open hands, fully outstretched with air. … Feel every tiny little joint fill up with this nourishment! When your arm and hand are filled to a satisfactory level, notice the difference between this arm and the other. … Does it feel bigger? Heavier? Wider? Longer? Any sensation is fine! Just observe it and appreciate it. … When you're ready, repeat this process on your own with your other arm and hand.

Notice that your body now has two full legs and arms and a dense abdomen. Your person balloon needs a fully inflated head too. On your next in-breath, imagine filling your head with fresh air, starting by your face. … Send air to the muscles in your cheeks … around your mouth … make sure you send an equal amount to both sides so they're equally relaxed and balanced! Send air around your eyes, eyelashes, eyebrows, and mouth. … What is the mouth of your person balloon expressing? What is the entire face expressing: peace, joy, stillness, openness, or curiosity? Decide if you want your person balloon to have ears inflated or closer to your head! When you're ready, fill your entire head with air so you have a nice head full of air and oxygen, one that fits perfectly with the body of your person balloon. … Take a minute to survey the whole of your creation, sensing what it's like to live in a person balloon-like body!

Now become aware of all the other person balloons around you! It's like being at a fair. … Everyone's person balloon is similar and different. … We are all full of air and water, and we all have a heart and similar insides. Our person balloons may have different sizes and colors and different facial expressions, but in the end, there are more similarities between us than differences. … Feel how you are one of many, and how the presence of others around you makes this group colorful, joyful, and interesting. I will count backward from 3 to 1 and when I get to 1, we will all open our eyes. 3, 2, 1.

Discussion Questions

For all discussions, these questions are simply a jumping-off point and a way to trigger curiosity. Feel free to choose what works best for your group, and remind them that these questions are just to help them reflect on the experience; we do not expect them to always have an answer right then and there.

- *How many of you could feel some air filling up different parts of your body?*
- *Where did you feel the greatest amount of air? Any guesses on which side of the lungs is bigger?*
- *Which colors were your lung balloons?*
- *Aside from the respiratory airways, what was the easiest part of your body to fill up with air?*
- *How was it to fill up your head, for example?*

- *Did you notice anything in particular about your face? What was your expression?*
- *What was it like to think of yourself as being part of a person balloon fair?*
- *Is it helpful to remember that we are more alike than different?*

Summary
It was fun to become person balloons with all of you today! This week, I invite you to notice your breath in a new way and see if you can purposely fill yourself with refreshing oxygen when you are feeling tired or down. As you notice your breath this week, remember that each and every person around you is breathing too—the same air is all around us and is the substance that connects us all.

Youth Variation
Young people really enjoy the option of being any living creature. They are so full of imagination and creativity that it may be more exciting to them to imagine being a penguin-shaped balloon. The exercise can be introduced as mentally playing with air! More examples and photos of animals' different respiratory systems can be given in the introduction. Participants can be instructed early in the process to pay careful attention because they will have to choose one of the creatures discussed and their breathing characteristic. It is easiest if the creatures discussed all have arms and legs, but sometimes children's favorite animal is a marine mammal, in which case they can imagine that fins are like legs since they allow mobility. If you use the example of a whale, you may also wish to add a sentence in the introduction stating that different creatures have their breathing opening at different places on their body, like the top of their head for a whale or everywhere on the skin for an amphibian, and to adjust accordingly.

With young people, it is preferable to facilitate every step of the process, even if it means repeating the exact same instructions twice, such as "inflating" each arm. In this case, the sentence "repeat on your own" in the script would be replaced.

A Garden of Toes

Words of wisdom: "Toes will always be at the end of your feet, but at the start of your journey."—Anthony T. Hincks

Intention: Engage people in an amusing metaphor, which helps to sustain focus on the sensations in their toes and to delve deeper into a meditative state.

Props: Yoga mattress, towel, or blanket for each participant to lie down on the floor in a circle.

Time: 20–30 minutes

Overview
Participants are placed in a circle with everyone's feet in the center and invited to imagine they are creating a garden of toes. Fascinating facts about the feet are shared (Spanne, 2015).

Facilitation
How much do your feet contribute to your life? How would your day-to-day existence be changed by the loss of even one toe? (Take participants' comments). *So life would be quite different, and our feet are precious, yet our society gives them very little TLC. Shoes are often fashionable rather than comfortable; we're often willing to sacrifice our feet to pain to look a certain way, and rarely do we realize these are living cells and crucial parts of our body. Feet are fascinating! The bones in our feet start off as cartilage in newborns and progressively harden until the age of 21 years old. They contain 26 bones each, almost a quarter of all the bones in our body! Your feet take an average of 8,000–10,000 steps for you in a day, which can be the equivalent of four trips around the world in a lifetime! Do they deserve some appreciation? Today we will get acquainted with our feet and the detailed sensations that arise in that area of our body.*

Let's start by sitting comfortably, closing our eyes, and taking three slow, deep breaths. Get your entire body to settle on your chair or mat, slowing down to stillness. Bring awareness to your feet. See if you can observe them as if this was something you had never seen before, with gentle curiosity and intrigue about what these "things" are and what they feel like. The design of feet is quite complex … study them as if you were an architect examining a wondrous construction. Feet allow our body to stand upright and even balance on one foot while we take a step and shift all our weight through the air. How can that small mass of tissue be the foundation of such stability in movement? Sense the experience of having feet, their general shape, length, width, and density. Notice they are at the end of a long, stick-like body.

Bring your awareness to one foot of your choice. Right now, is it exactly the same as the other, or does it feel bigger, smaller, or shorter … even if you know logically that both feet are roughly the same, muscle tightness may make one of them feel quite different. Notice the differences and keep on breathing slowly without forcing. Again, choose one foot to focus on. Try to feel the different parts of your feet and ankles. Notice how your heel feels hard and solid, how it attaches to your ankle and leg. Feel the skin on top of your foot and how different it is than the skin on the bottom. Imagine feeling the bones in your feet, their location, beginning, and end. If your feet have a certain volume, feel the density inside your tissue. You may sense something hard in some areas and something soft elsewhere. If there's any discomfort, try not moving anything for now, just take notice of it and breathe through it; it might fade away just with the power of breath. Take a minute to observe and feel some gratefulness for your foot. If you find your mind wandering, gently bring it back.

Now take another deep breath and imagine sending air all the way down to each toe of that foot. You can start with either side of your foot, sending air either to your big toe or to your little toe. Then, slowly, meticulously, make sure you fully inflate and feel each toe, one by one, without rushing, in a three-dimensional way. Try to feel the flow of life in each toe, one after the other, noticing where they are bent, where they are humid, dry, or cracked, where there is some webbing. Notice if there is any soreness, blister, or discomfort. What surface is each toe touching (socks or floor)? Is there any pressure? Feel air moving on and in between your toes. What is it like to have a nail on top of each toe? When you've studied and relaxed one foot thoroughly, slowly zoom out slightly to view both feet. Notice the differences between the foot you just observed and the one you did not pay attention to. Compare sensations. Is one heavier? … Denser? … Longer? … Warmer? When you're ready, bring your awareness and curiosity to your other foot; it probably feels slightly different. Repeat the observation process on your own.

When both feet are relaxed, become aware of the many other toes around you, those of other people in this room! If we were in a cartoon movie and toes were like a plant or a flower, we could create a cute garden of toes! Imagine that you are a part of a beautiful whole. Sense people around you, who all have toes. Visualize that you are a part of a cartoon featuring a garden of toes. Our bodies are rooted in the ground, like plants, and we are immobile, silently alive. Feel the air flow around us in the entire room. Notice the sensations that this imagery triggers in your toes. Take a few minutes to enjoy this experience. In a few minutes, I will count backward from 3 to 1, and then we'll all slowly open our eyes, refreshed and ready to discuss our experiences. 3, 2, 1.

Discussion Questions

- *What was it like to attempt noticing the sensations in your feet and toes? Did you succeed in feeling each of your toes one by one? How about the skin on your feet? Did you notice differences? Did anyone feel the difference between areas with and without bones?*
- *Did you discover a part of your foot that was sore and that you may not have noticed before? What helped you handle the soreness?*

- *What differences did you observe between the first foot you relaxed and the foot that was not relaxed yet?*
- *Were you able to feel appreciation for your feet?*
- *How was the imagery of a garden of toes and what did that trigger?*
- *If this exercise was to have tweaked your experience of your feet, what might you think, feel, or do slightly differently?*

Summary

Today we gave some appreciation to our toes—10 little body parts that play a big role in our lives! This week, as you are walking around or standing still, see if you can bring some of that same attention and appreciation to your toes.

Youth Variation

While adults may remove their socks and shoes, it is often preferable to avoid this with children and let them keep their socks and shoes on. Depending on the size and age of the group, remaining dressed avoids incidents such as misplaced items, someone inadvertently taking the shoe of another, or a struggle in tying shoelaces. The facilitation script differs here in that instead of the moving air caressing the foot and inserting itself in between the toes, fairies are imagined tending to the garden of toes. Many adults who value imagination and creativity also really like this version. Fairies are then pictured going from toe to toe checking with their little hands for any blisters or injuries, examining nails, and even giving a loving hug to each toe. They are making sure, with gentle massages, that each toe is fully extended and oriented toward the sunlight high above. If you involve fairies, make sure to keep the focus on sensing the toes, and do not drift into a completely imaginary world.

The Touching Hand

Words of wisdom: "Sometimes, reaching out and taking someone's hand is the beginning of a journey. At other times, it is allowing another to take yours."—Vera Nazarian

Intention: Facilitate interoception and improved connection to the body by mindfully focusing on the sensation of touch.

Props: Chairs, tables, and enough space for one person to rest a hand on a table while the other, seated in front, respectfully touches it. Access to a sink or wet wipes.

Time: 20–30 minutes

Overview

After discussing interesting facts about hands, participants are invited to take a break to wash their hands and then to pair up with someone else they feel comfortable with. Participants will take turns exploring the other's hand and focusing on the sensation of touch. The eyes of everyone remain closed throughout the exercise in order to focus on sensing with touch. The "explorer" should be encouraged to give a gentle, light touch to their partner, and the owner of the hand (the "receiver") should remain still and focused on the experience of the subtle touch (this is important to emphasize with children). This exercise can be repeated at the following session and the roles reversed so that everyone gets a chance to have both experiences.

Facilitation

How much do we rely on our hands each day? Take a minute to think about everything your hands have done for you today. What sorts of things come to mind? (Take participants' comments). *Our hands are an integral part of our life—they help us write, wave hello, hold another's hand, put food in our mouth, and bring our loved ones close. Hands help nourish us and connect us to one another. They are a fascinating and complex part of our body.*

Did you know that there are 27 bones and 29 joints in each of your hands (Pathak, 2017)*? The muscles in your wrist and your forearm contract and stretch to allow your hands to move. Take a moment to extend one of your arms, with your palm facing down. Keep your arm steady and move your hand up so that your fingers point to the ceiling, and then move your fingers back down* (instructor demonstrates). *Feel the way that your forearm tightens and relaxes during this movement.*

Now bring your arm back down and direct your attention to your skin. The sensory receptors and nerves underneath your skin take in all kinds of information through your hands. They sense if something is hot, cold, rough, or soft, how heavy something is, and if something is moving. There is even some evidence to suggest that the nerve endings in your hand can conduct complex processing about the objects they touch—they "think" about the form, shape, and texture of the object, something scientists originally thought could happen only in the brain (Costandi, 2014)*! Now take your hands and rub them together—we will all rub our hands for about 20 seconds. … As you rub, notice all of those sensory receptors lighting up and sending signals to your brain. How do your hands feel? Do they feel tingly … energized … or warm?*

We are going to spend some time exploring hands and focusing on the sensation of touch. Before we begin, please go wash your hands or clean them with a wet wipe. As you return to your seat, please partner up with a person you feel comfortable with.

Have a seat in a comfortable position facing your partner, and decide who will be the explorer and who will be the receiver. Once you have decided, take a moment to settle in. When you are ready, take a deep breath in and out, bringing awareness to your body. Feel the weight of your hands on the table or in your lap. Take another deep breath in, channeling the fresh air down your arms and into your hands, all the way to each fingertip. Now the receivers can place their hands palm down on the table, close their eyes, and focus on the sensations of their hands. The explorers can use one finger and slowly, gently touch the hand of their partner. Begin at the wrist and go slowly, gently down each finger. Keep your touch light—see if you hover your fingertip right above their hand, just barely touching their skin, as if you were a feather. As you move your finger across their hand, take notice of the texture of their skin, the small bumps of their knuckles, and each crease at their joints. Are there places where the skin is rough, or where it is especially smooth? See if you can feel each and every hair that you pass over. … Pretend that you are like an explorer of a new land, experiencing and noting each and every aspect. The knuckles might feel like little mountains, and the creases could be like small, connected streams. As you reach the fingernail, notice how the texture changes. What does it feel like to you? Go just past the fingernail to the edge, and feel the pressure of the edge on your finger as you go across it. As you go back across the hand, be mindful of the thousands of pores you are passing over, just a fraction of the millions of pores on our bodies. Our pores act like little chimneys for warmth to escape, keeping our bodies at the perfect temperature. When you go across the hand, see if you can sense the minuscule streams of warmth coming out from these little chimneys.

If your mind begins to wander, gently bring it back. As the explorers run their fingers across your hand, receivers focus on the experience of your hand being touched. See how it feels to be touched on your hand … your fingers … your fingernails. Do you experience different sensations in different parts of your hand? Notice how the pressure of the explorer's touch might change ever so slightly as the explorer moves down your fingers. Try to trace the slow movement of the explorer, drawing a map in your mind of the path. As the explorer moves across your hand, sensory receptors light up as the finger approaches and fade as the finger moves on. Imagine the explorer making a path of light as they move around your hand.

After the explorer has had a chance to explore each finger, receivers can flip their hand over so it is palm up. Receivers, check in with your hand—does the table feel different to the top of your hand than it did to your palm? Take a moment to rest and relax your hands, loosening the muscles in your wrist and letting your fingers fall open. Explorers, take one finger and slowly, gently touch the hand of your partner, beginning at the wrist. Move around the curve of the palm, going down the fingers on the outside. … As you come to the fingertip, remember that this fingerprint pattern is completely unique, belonging only to your partner—you will never feel the same one again. Come back up to the wrist, and cross the valley of the palm to the middle fingers. You might follow the creases of the palm, like curvy, well-worn trails, or you might forge your own path. Notice the dips and the bumps as you move across the hand, seeing if you can feel the slight indent of each crease that you pass over. You might even be able to feel where bones and veins are. What do these feel like? Isn't it amazing that we can know what we are touching without even looking at it?

Receivers, continue to trace the explorers' movements across your hand. Notice the differences in the sensations of touch on this side of your hand, in comparison to the top of your hand. See if you can sense the temperature of the explorers' fingers—perhaps they feel warm, perhaps they feel cold. Does the feeling of their fingers change as they go from your wrist, across your palm, and down your fingers? Explorers, take this time to explore your last finger, and return your hands to your lap. Can you feel the absence of your partner's hand on your fingertip? Receivers, see if you can locate the last place that the explorers touched, remembering how it felt to have a finger there and noticing its absence. When you are ready, take a deep breath in, and out, and open your eyes.

Discussion Questions

- *How was it for you to pay so much attention to your hands? How often do you pay this much attention to your hands?*
- *Explorers: What did you notice about your partner's hand? How many different textures did you encounter?*
- *Receivers: How did it feel to have someone touching your hand? If you had your eyes closed, what were you picturing in your mind?*
- *How might this exercise change the way you interact with or think about your hands?*

Summary

Thank you all for being open to engaging in an exercise with a partner. Sometimes it can feel a bit vulnerable to do that! Our hands are tools for connection in so many ways. They allow us to reach out to others for a hug, handshake, or high five, pass objects or gifts between people, open doors to our home, and wave to our friends. This week, see if you can notice and feel your hands when you connect with others.

Youth Variation

While the partner aspect of this exercise can be helpful in creating a mindfulness community and introducing mindfulness in our interactions with others, partnering up may be too distracting for some young children. In this case, this exercise can be tweaked to be an individual activity. During the exploration, the child can explore one of their own hands with their other. After exploration, the individual can move to sensing and use a paintbrush to brush different areas of their hands, focusing on the sensation of the paintbrush on their skin.

Orbiting the Eyes

Words of wisdom: "Since we cannot change reality, let us change the eyes which see reality."—Nikos Kazantzakis

Intention: Improve the connection to one's body and physical manifestations of emotions by engaging in observation and sensing of our eyes (see Figure 6.2).

Props: Visual depicting different parts of eyes; an object to visually observe.

Time: 20–30 minutes

Overview

The eyes are heavily involved in everything we do. The information they collect represents a large portion of the sensory information that enters the brain. Eyes are also significantly connected with emotions. Each human emotion is associated with a unique pattern of muscular contraction around the eyes. Trauma and fear, for example, recruit tiny muscles to zoom in intently on the threatening stimulus

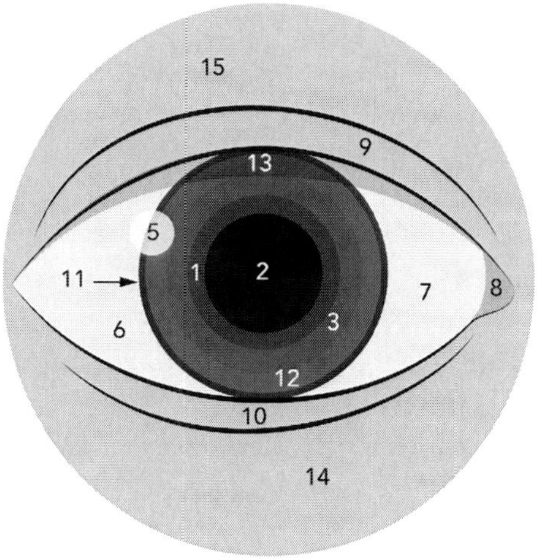

Figure 6.2. Many Interesting Areas of the Eye Can Be Sensed And Observed as if Noting the Sections in a Coloring Book.

(show photos of eye muscles engaged with anger, sadness, and fear). *From an evolutionary standpoint, these tiny muscles are supposed to be activated only occasionally, as the large peripheral vision muscles are better equipped for constant, default daily use. Unfortunately, our modern lifestyle has hijacked this program by recruiting these tiny muscles to focus for long hours on screens, computers, and iPhones. This exercise is focused on attempting to feel eye muscles and notice their effect on our eyeballs. We then expand to how our eyes change with different emotional states.*

Facilitation

Those of us with sight use our eyes each day to gather information about the world around us. We use our eyes to read, find friends and family in a crowd, and take in beautiful nature scenes. What else do we use our eyes for? (Facilitator takes a few ideas from the group).

Even though we might feel like our vision is automatic, the act of sight is actually quite complicated! Our eyes control how much light we let in by changing the size of the pupil—at nighttime, the pupil is much larger in order to let in more light and to help us see in the dark. After the light comes through the pupil, it hits millions of photoreceptor cells in each eye that detect patterns of light, shapes, and colors. However, because our eyes are curved, this information actually comes in upside down! The brain then makes sense of these different signals and turns the image right side up, transforming it into the cohesive picture that we see in our mind. Our eyes are almost constantly moving, so this process happens hundreds of thousands of times a day (Irwin, 2001).

We are going to see if we can observe the experience of having eyes. Let's begin by grounding ourselves in our breath. Take a deep breath in, pause, and breathe out. As you take your next breath in, allow your gaze to relax and soften, looking wherever feels most comfortable for you. For most people, the eye's resting place is a few feet in front of them. Notice how your eyes feel. Are they tired? Dry? Moist? Are your eyelids drooping, or are your eyes wide open? See if you can feel the weight of your eyelid on your eye. Do you feel some muscles that may be overused?

Reengage your gaze, and without moving your head, look up. How does this sensation feel? Can you feel the muscles around your eyes tightening? Where are your eyebrows, your eyelids? Did they move up as well? Keep your gaze there and notice what physical sensations come up for you. You might experience discomfort or straining, or you may enjoy the experience of looking up. Now direct your gaze downward and notice what shifts. How do your eyes feel now? Do they feel heavier, or more relaxed? Notice where your eyelids and eyebrows have moved. How does it feel to look down?

Without moving your head, look to your right, noticing what kinds of muscles this engages. Can you see a faint outline of your nose? Look to your left and notice the other side of your nose. Continue to move your eyes in different directions, noticing the differences of what you see and feel with each movement. ... See if you can notice the presence of air on your eyes. How does this change when you move your eyes to the left or to the right?

Return your eyes to a comfortable rest position and continue to observe how they feel. If you find your mind wandering, gently bring it back. Do your eyes feel different from when you started? Notice how the muscles around your eyes feel. Are they strained? Tight? Relaxed? The muscles around our eyes are the most active muscles in our bodies, partially because they are involved in blinking, which we do approximately 17 times every minute, which totals about 5 million times per year! Blink quickly and notice the sensation. Can you feel your eyelids cover your eyes? Can you feel your muscles moving? Blink again, slowly this time, tracking the movement of your eyelid and your eye muscles ... see if you can detect the motion of your bottom eyelid as well, and notice where your eyelids are meeting.

The muscles around our eyes also focus our vision. Choose an object that intrigues you on the opposite side of the room (facilitator can also hold something up to focus on), and actively focus your eyes on this object. ... Notice the subtle changes in your eyes as you focus. Do your eyes move? Which muscles are tensing? Allow your eyes to relax ... let your vision go blurry. How is this different?

Finally, these muscles also move our eyes and the surrounding area to show different emotions. Smile and notice how your eyes change shape. What muscles are engaged? Does this change what you see? Notice where your eyelids, eyebrows, and eyeballs are. I will name a few more emotions ... each time, allow that emotion to live on your face ... notice what shape your eyes make and what muscles are moving to make this shape. Sadness ... Anger ... Fear ... Exhaustion ... Surprise ... Joy.

Take a deep breath in. As you breathe out, allow your eyes to relax once more, melting the tension away. Close your eyes as you continue to relax them. Remain still and sense your eyes just as they are right now in this room. What kind of emotions or feelings come up for you now? Just observe. Do you feel peaceful, at ease, or calm? Allow your eyelids to continue to become heavier as you sink into this moment of tranquility. Notice how your eyes, eyelids, eyebrows, and facial muscles feel as you breathe deeply in, and deeply out. Just sense your eyes ... observe their roundedness and how close they are to one another. Feel grateful for their presence. ... Take a few more deep breaths. ... When you are ready, open your eyes.

Discussion Questions

- *What did you notice about your eyes that surprised you?*
- *Were you able to sense the different muscles moving when you moved your gaze up, down, left, and right? How did that feel?*

- *What came up for you when you moved your eyes in accordance with your emotions? What kind of shapes did your eyes make?*
- *How did it feel to relax your eyes? What position felt more comfortable for your eyes?*

Summary

Before today, did you realize all the different sensations associated with your eyes? This week, try and take note of this—notice when your eyes are squinty and observe what is happening with that precious part of your body (e.g., Is it sunny? Are you irritated? Tired? Dehydrated?). Then try relaxing the muscles around your eyes and see if you can take better care of your precious eyes.

Youth Variation

When performing this exercise with children, it may be helpful to have an object or a picture for them to focus on in the beginning of the exercise. This must be something that is intriguing and interesting for them to look at, or else children will likely become distracted. After a few minutes, have them close their eyes and just focus on sensing that body part.

Mysterious Mouth

Words of wisdom: "A smile is a curve that sets everything straight."—Phyllis Diller

Intention: Help people notice the experience of having a mouth, and observe all the different parts and processes the mouth is involved in.

Props: Yoga mattress, towel, or blanket for each participant to lie down on the floor in a circle.

Time: 20–30 minutes

Overview

This meditation reviews the different parts of the mouth, teeth, tongue, gums, palate, saliva, and their fascinating aspects, and then invites participants to focus on observing how it feels to have a mouth.

Facilitation

Today we are going to talk about something that we use every single day. In fact, I am using it right now—can anyone guess what it is? (Take a few guesses and validate each response). *It is the mouth!*

The mouth accomplishes the incredible feat of cutting, grinding, and chewing food without biting the moving muscle of the tongue—it's like a refined machine. How many movements does a mouth make during a meal? And how frequently do people bite their tongue? That's a pretty small percentage! We use our mouth every day to eat, drink, breathe, and speak—activities that are crucial for our survival and social connection. Inside of our mouths, we have our gums, teeth, and tongue. Our teeth are all different shapes and sizes to help us chew our food. Each tooth is surrounded by enamel, which is even stronger than our bones! Our tongues are actually muscles and are constantly working to move saliva around even when we are asleep. The pattern of taste buds on our tongue is unique—much like fingerprints, each person has their own "tongue print." Our tongue also allows us to make the different noises of letters and words to help us communicate with others—it bends and twists to change the way air comes out of our mouth. Try saying your name out loud slowly, noticing how your tongue moves within your mouth and how your lips change shape. (Give participants a few seconds to say their names aloud). *Our mouth can move in the way that it does because of the powerful surrounding muscles in the jaw. The largest jaw muscle, called the masseter, can crush with a force of 55 pounds!*

Let's take some time to explore and appreciate our mouths. Find a comfortable position and begin to slow down your breath. Take a deep breath in through your nose, and out through your mouth. Take another deep breath in … pause … and then breathe out. Feel free to close your eyes and continue to focus on your breathing. How does your breath feel as it comes out your mouth? Can you feel it on the inside of your mouth or brushing past your lips? How do your lips feel? Are they tingly or warm? Does your mouth feel dry after breathing out through your mouth? Now close your mouth and continue to breathe in and out through your nose. Feel the moisture of the saliva returning to your mouth. Observe the sheer open space inside of your mouth. Is there air in that space? Do you feel the movement of air? Our mouth, nose, and ear passageways are all connected, so you may be able to detect the movement of your breath even when your mouth is closed. Notice where you feel the air moving—is it in the open space of your mouth, or the back of your throat?

Notice where your tongue is in your mouth—is it touching the roof of your mouth, or is it tucked at the bottom? Pretend the tip of your tongue is like an explorer, and investigate the different shapes and textures of your mouth. Scan your teeth one by one … try to notice the different sizes of your teeth. How do the sides feel in comparison to the bottoms or tops of your teeth? There are no nerves in the teeth themselves, so you might notice that you cannot feel your tongue on your teeth. Move upward or downward from your teeth to feel your gums. Are your gums warm or cool? Are they inflamed …

bumpy … or flat? Let your tongue become still. Try to relax your tongue and notice where in your mouth it likes to rest.

If your mind has started to wander, gently bring it back. Now try swallowing a few times, observing all of the different movements of your tongue and throat. How does it feel to swallow? Are both sides of your throat swallowing equally? Sometimes neck tensions or accidents can skew that process. Check in with the muscles in your jaw and your neck that help you swallow. Are they tight? Is your jaw clenched? In your next few out-breaths, focus on relaxing those muscles and letting go of the tension … as you become more relaxed, notice where your tongue has moved (the natural resting place of the tongue is behind the upper teeth).

Our mouth also helps us express gratitude, happiness, or excitement by smiling. Scientists have always known that we smile when we are happy, but research now shows that smiling can actually make it easier to feel happy (see Figure 6.3)! As soon as we begin to smile, our brain releases chemicals that make us feel relaxed, lower our heart rate and blood pressure, and lift our mood. The brain likes to be congruent with the muscles, so if the muscles show a happy face, then the brain tries to follow, and vice versa. Give yourself a big, genuine smile and allow yourself to be filled with positivity and gratitude for all the things our mouth does for us. Take a few seconds to just observe and feel that inside of you.

Smiling is also contagious—when we see someone else smiling, it makes us want to smile too! Open up your eyes, look at everyone smiling around you, and notice how your smile grows.

Discussion Questions

- *How was it to notice the different parts of your mouth? Did you notice anything new about your mouth that you had not noticed before?*
- *Were you able to relax your tongue and your jaw muscles? If so, did you find that process easy or difficult? How did it feel to have those muscles relaxed?*
- *Were you able to feel appreciation for your mouth?*
- *How did it feel to smile at the end of the meditation? Did you notice any differences? Did you find it easy or difficult to stop smiling when you looked around and saw others smiling?*

Summary

I am still smiling from watching you all smile! It was a beautiful sight. This week, see if you can experiment with changing your mood by changing the shape of your mouth—try relaxing your jaw and see if you feel more peaceful, or try smiling and see if it lifts your mood. You may also consider speaking up more when you have

Figure 6.3. Research Shows That We Are More Likely to Feel Happy When We Activate the Smile Muscles.

something nice to say, and contribute to others smiling more often. As stated by William Arthur Ward, "Feeling gratitude and not expressing it, is like wrapping a present and not giving it!"

Youth Variation

This exercise does not require much variation to be used with children. The inclusion of specific actions (e.g., exploring teeth, swallowing) helps children remain engaged and focused on the activity. Depending on the age of the youth, the language used in the discussion about the mouth may need to be simplified. This exercise also goes well with the laughing meditation (in Chapter 4).

The Annoyance Test

Words of wisdom: "When we are no longer able to change a situation, we are challenged to change ourselves."—Viktor Frankl

Props: Audio recording of a car alarm.

Time: 20–30 minutes

Overview

Invite participants to engage in a review of which body part or sensation is fascinating to them and why. For some it is feelings of warmth, for others it is vibrations, for others still it is the experience of melting tension in certain muscles or the impression of expansion in their lungs or toes. The test involves being exposed to an annoying sound, such as a car alarm. There can be two mindful responses: remaining calm and connected to multiple other body parts in spite of the audio recording, or losing oneself in the soundscape without judging, labeling, or reacting. Participants practice not getting overwhelmed by the sound reaching their ears, especially considering the ears are a relatively small body part compared to the rest of the body.

Facilitation

Let's review the sensations you like to observe in your body. What are your favorite body parts to scan, study, sense, and observe? (Take many participant ideas).

Your test today will be to remain composed and calm in the face of an annoying sound: can anyone guess what that may be?(Listen to participants' guesses.) … *Yes, it is a car alarm.*

We will start by meditating calmly and finding some inner peace and a sense of acceptance, then I will let you know when the sound is about to start. You have two options in facing the sound: 1) Be 100% mindful and accepting of the sound, without labeling, judging, or being annoyed by it … just noticing its presence, absence, bathing in the cornucopia of what arises around you and far from you, and the space between the different notes, observing their layers and nuances; or 2) focus on other sensorial experiences of your body, acknowledging that sounds are there, but choosing to have your mind dwell elsewhere in some other fascinating body part of your choice. You can even alternate between the two options, whatever fits for you.

After we get settled, I will play the sound for 1 or 2 minutes at a lower volume and help you through the process of remaining peaceful. Then I may increase it to a medium volume, and let you use your own strategies. So find a comfortable position … close your eyes … and take a calming breath. Find your center … your inner peace … joy … acceptance. Enjoy the present moment, how it is perfect just as it is … with people around you … a chair to support you … a fascinating body that allows you to come here and enjoy these meetings … breathe and savor … appreciate your body as it is right now. Notice whatever sounds arise just now … intensify your feeling of joy and peace by imagining you can breathe it in.

I will now start the recording. Challenge yourself to control how much of the sound enters your mind, and control your emotional reactions to it … different emotions can make the experience much more or less annoying. Notice the judgments and comments your mind is tempted to make, as if they were leaves blowing in the wind, without giving them too much attention. ... Notice how there is still silence just around your body, with other sounds coexisting in the space. ... The sound is emitted several feet away from you—contrast that with the silence in and around you ... or allow your mind to dwell in helpful places in your body and to marvel on how everything is still as beautiful as before. ... I will now let you complete the rest on your own.

(Allow one more minute; keep in mind that we want participants to succeed, so in case of doubt, it's best to reduce the volume to end with an experience of competency.)

Discussion Questions

- *Were you able to keep your inner world peaceful?*
- *Which strategies did you use to keep the sound out and tolerable?*
- *How did you use your fascinating body parts to help you in this situation?*

Summary

You all faced the challenge of being in the face of an experience often considered annoying, and found strategies to remain anchored in your own peace of mind and observing state! Try to see if you can replicate that this week! Congratulations on facing the test bravely! Give yourselves a hand!

Youth Variation

No variation necessary.

CHAPTER SEVEN

Nature Mindfulness Meditations

Creating Experiences of Peaceful Connection, Belonging, Empathy, and Gratitude

This collection of belonging and gratefulness meditations represents a higher level of difficulty. Previous collections invited participants to explore their own experiences, but in this chapter, participants are encouraged to attain these deep states of consciousness more rapidly and then to expand their awareness beyond their individual realm. They are invited to progressively connect with the experience of being part of a group of people who are sharing similar states and purposes. A sense of belonging can emerge when they feel part of an ensemble or landscape that is much richer than the focus on the individual experience. Out of this expansion comes a greater sense of harmony, recognition that others are precious, and openness to taking the perspective of others. In fact, it could be said that "each person we interact with provides a doorway into a new world" (Stahl & Goldstein, 2010, p. 157).

The exercises presented in this chapter are organized in an increasing level of difficulty, offering a progression from a simple awareness of self and others to the awareness of forming a greater whole, where one can appreciate the complex, delicate systems of life. This series progressively brings forth qualities of humanness, compassion, dignity, and belonging, and ends with a challenge: can we sustain these qualities of humanness and feel emotions without joining, reacting, or being overwhelmed? This challenge is the culmination of all the exercises featured in this book and allows participants to test their skills of remaining calm and compassionate in the face of a profoundly difficult experience.

An Important Dot

Words of wisdom: "Be a rainbow in someone else's cloud."—Maya Angelou

Intention: Cultivate a double awareness of our own being and of those around us forming a whole.

Time: 20–30 minutes

Props: Dot art nature images with multiple roundish components (see Figure 7.1). With young children, plan on showing five or six of such colorful illustrations to ensure they will like at least one. In addition to dot art illustrations, zoomed photos of animals such as the enlarged eye of a dragonfly, the colorful back of a fish, or the leg of an octopus allow participants to have a fun guessing exchange. Several of these types of images are available in the *National Geographics for Kids* magazine.

Overview

The facilitator asks participants if they tend to focus on whole pictures, or only portions of what they see. The group then discusses busy people's tendencies to have a narrower focus. The exercise of becoming a small item that will later belong to a whole is introduced without mentioning any specific details in order to keep the mystery and facilitate the process of simply being in the flow of present time experience. Each one of us is a dot in a bigger picture. We often contribute and receive more when we are aware of being part of a group. A small portion of this meditation was featured in a professional DVD (Beaudoin, 2013).

Figure 7.1. Example of a "Dot Illustration".

Facilitation

(Adult beginning) *Today we will experience our simple uniqueness and connect it with the uniqueness of others. Our mind often needs to simplify the huge amount of information we are exposed to. While ideally we could hold both a dot of information and a big-picture view, we often tend to be oblivious to the wider angle. This may be particularly true in individualistic societies, or in communities where people's lives are dominated by busyness, deadlines, and being caught in their thinking.* (All ages) *Does this small element of an image have any meaning for you on its own?* (Show dragon-fly eye illustration). *Can you guess what it is? Most people can't guess what it is. How about this one? Can you guess what it is? If I show you the bigger picture, however, it suddenly becomes a meaningful and even important part of this image. It shifts the value of the small piece. Similarly, as people, we hold great value as a member of a community and have a much richer experience when we hold our own self-awareness in combination with an awareness of others.*

So let's try an exercise in sensing our own and others' bodies in a unique way. You will become a part of something mysterious.

Start by closing your eyes and sitting comfortably straight. Take a slow, deep breath through your nose. Take a few breaths like this, trying to slow your inhale and exhale. … As you slow down your breath, you might notice some parts of your body feeling a little heavier. … Find the part of your body that feels heaviest and focus on those sensations. … Feel the lethargy seeping into different areas of your body. … Notice how you are becoming more and more still, on the chair supporting you. … You are feeling so still that you can almost become like a pebble.

Imagine that you are a beautiful pebble. Feel like a pebble. What color might you be? Do you have many different colors… on the front or the back of you? … Are you a gentle brown, a sunny yellow, a joyful red, or a peaceful grey? … Imagine yourself as a colorful pebble. … You are small and tough … it doesn't matter if there is weight on you as you just sink in the sand and then come back out another time, still the same pebble. You are breathing in and out so gently and slowly that many observers might not notice the movement. … This breathing movement is like a gentle wind over the pebble, or like the water of a brook flowing peacefully toward a lake. … If your mind starts to wander, gently bring it back. … As you are sitting here, feeling like a pebble, become aware that there are other beautiful pebbles around you. … Luckily, you are part of something much bigger than just yourself; you belong to a community of pebbles and together you all form something great! … You can be part of that group of special pebbles that contribute to the gurgling sound of a cascade, but without the others, there is no cascade. … You can be a colorful pebble on a rocky riverbank, but without the others, you are just a lost rock. … You can be a pebble at the bottom of the ocean, forming a solid bed that many creatures enjoy, but without the other rocks, there is no solid bed. … Alternatively, you can be a pebble in a small city, a pebble that has been used as an important feature of a decorative mosaic on the ground, created by a talented artist. ... Without you, the ground is uneven, but without the others, no artistic image can exist. ... The sum of all of you creates an amazing whole, rich with many possibilities. ... Be aware that all the pebbles around you are similar to you and also different ... they each contribute something really special. ... All pebbles are valuable. Even the pebble who is unstable and moving all the time, or the pebble with a pointy edge, or the pebble with less color than you. ... Just as being part of a team allows for a more fun game, being part of any community contributes a lot to your days. ... Take a moment to feel grateful for this group of pebbles you belong to right now;... feel the presence of the group and how big it is. ... Some people feel safer or more important when they include everyone around them in their awareness. ... See if you can feel small in yourself and big with your group at the same time, and feel grateful for that possibility. ... I will count backward from 5 to 1, and when I reach 1, we will all open our eyes.

Discussion Questions

For all discussions, these questions are simply a jumping-off point and a way to trigger curiosity. Feel free to choose what works best for your group, and remind them that these questions are just to help them reflect on the experience; we do not expect them to always have an answer right then and there.

- *How many of you managed to feel like a pebble?*
- *What were the colors of your pebble? Was it round or did it have a special shape?*
- *Raise your hand if you felt in a river or in an ocean. Raise your hand if you felt in a mosaic. Was anyone part of something else?*
- *How did breathing feel, like the wind or water?*
- *Did you like being a pebble? What did you like about it? How many of you felt the presence of the other pebbles around you? Did you like belonging to a group?*
- *Did you feel small (in yourself) and big (with the group) at the same time? What did you discover about being in a group? Raise your hand if you felt some gratefulness to have a community as opposed to being a lonely pebble.*
- *Why are you grateful to have this group? What does it make possible that you could not do if you were alone? For example, do we laugh more or less when we are part of a group? How is playing alone versus with others different? Can you think of any other differences? Do we have more or fewer solutions*

to problems? Are there more inventions when someone is alone on a deserted island or in a society of people?

- *How much beauty in life do we miss by focusing on a small point of information?*

Summary

I hope you all enjoyed becoming a pebble today, one that is unique and part of a group at the same time. Find moments to be "pebblish" this week, just being in the present moment, feeling unique, strong, valuable, and part of a community. Sometimes we receive support from being in a community. Other times, as Maya Angelou says, we can "be a rainbow in someone else's cloud" and contribute an important dot of color in "the image" of that day.

Youth Variation

The youth version differs mostly at the beginning and the end. When facilitating with youth, you can skip the first paragraph of the adult facilitation, and begin instead with an exciting announcement: "*Today, we will talk about the mystery of dots and how each one of us is an important dot in something bigger! We often just focus on our own self, but if we were to think of the bigger group that we belong to, we would see things very differently. It is the difference between seeing just a little bit of something versus seeing a lot of something. For example, who can guess what this is?*" The facilitator can show a series of enlarged miniature segments of known creatures and have children guess what is the whole creature. The rest of the facilitation is the same as for adults. The facilitator can also invite children to draw themselves as a pebble and to imagine what their group would look like if it was a riverbed. Some of this meditation was facilitated with very young children for the professional film *From Bullies to Buddies* (Beaudoin, 2013).

Tide Pool

Words of wisdom: "There is a deep interconnectedness of all life on earth, from the tiniest organisms, to the largest ecosystems, and absolutely between each person."—Bryant McGill

Intention: Recognize and celebrate the uniqueness of every being and the important role that each being plays in the community.

Time: 20–30 minutes

Props: This meditation includes some slight movement—it would be helpful to have a yoga mat on which to lie down with arms and legs open like a starfish, and a meditation cushion or a chair to sit on as a creature propped up by a rock. Facilitators will also need pictures of tide pools.

Overview

Using the metaphor of a tide pool, the facilitator creates an experience of sensing the presence of others. In this exercise, the facilitator discusses tide pool creatures, and then induces a state of meditation where each participant chooses and embodies one of the creatures. Embodying a creature, which is not perceived as thinking, often allows people (especially busy adults) to bypass their mental activity and dwell in their sensory experiences. The ocean breath discussed in Chapter 4 can easily be added to this exercise to create a lovely experience. As people are connecting to their senses, they are invited to widen the scope of their awareness to include the presence of others around them.

Facilitation

Today we will use tide pools as a metaphor for our experience. Tide pools may seem simple, but they are actually quite complex and have a lot to teach us. Imagining and embodying the experience of other creatures sometimes allows our brain to enter new, unique states that we didn't even know we could achieve. Let's look at these photos to refresh our memories. Which creature stands out to you? Which might be your favorite? (Invite participants to share which creature is most intriguing to them). *These small pools of ocean life are formed by the tides, pulled in and out by the gravitational power of the moon and the sun. These creatures live together, contributing to the life of the tide pool in a unique and crucial way. For example, seaweed has a very important job—as water retreats and the sunlight reaches into the pool, the seaweed produces oxygen for the rest of the living beings in the tide pool. Without seaweed, other sea creatures would not get the nutrients they need. Some seaweed, called algae, even lives inside other creatures to make sure they get the oxygen they need. Anemones in the tide pool provide a protective home for the algae, and in turn take in the oxygen the algae produces. Anemones are interesting as they have adapted to the changing environment of the tide pool. When the tide retreats, anemones curl into themselves, covering their fragile bodies with seashells and pebbles to protect themselves from the sun. Did you all notice the starfish in the tide pool? Starfish are "keystone" animals—without them, the fragile ecosystem within this tide pool would fall apart. Without their steady diet of mussels and snails, the smaller creatures in the tide pool would completely consume the seaweed and drive out other life-forms. Hundreds of tiny tube feet allow the starfish to move around within the pool and to grip onto the rock as the tide comes in and out.*

The creatures of the tide pool rely not only on each other but also on their surroundings. They use the large boulders to find somewhere to make a home, and they use the small pebbles for protection. They need the sun to warm them and to provide the light required for photosynthesis. They must have the moon pull the tides in and out again to maintain the water in the pool and receive a renewal of ocean nutrients. Everything in this tide pool—big and small—is connected. If someone removes even one creature, the entire community is affected. Together, they can use the unique gifts and contributions of each member to thrive.

We are going to create our own tide pool community here. To begin, settle in your seat and close your eyes. Bring your attention to your breath. As you breathe in and out, notice how your diaphragm rises and falls. Your breath is like the ocean tide, flowing in … and out … in … and out (this is a good place to insert the ocean breath of Chapter 4). *Our breath and the tide follow the same natural rhythm. As you become connected to the cadence of the tides, choose one tide pool creature as a source of inspiration for today. You might be a starfish, a sea cucumber, an anemone, seaweed, or a sea urchin. As you continue to breathe with the tide, your body may begin to feel heavier. Allow yourself to sink into the experience of your chosen tide pool creature. … If you are like a starfish, you may feel your limbs start becoming tingly, stretched, or heavy. … If you are embodying an urchin, you may find yourself feeling like a sphere safely propped against a solid surface. … If you have become a hermit crab, you may have the sensation of being protected and hugged by your chair, like you have a shell to call home. … Feel the slight movements of the air around you, like the water that gently ripples through the tide pool with the wind … which part of you is touching the moving air or water, is it your skin, the hardened surfaces of you, or tiny little hairs? Focus on the sensation of air in this part of your body. If you are like seaweed, you may find yourself feeling light and swaying with the slight movements of air around you. … If you have transformed into a sea cucumber, you might feel like a sponge, soaking up the air and the peaceful environment we have created. … Take a few more breaths, in and out again, as your sea creature. See if you can hear the sounds of water swirling around you or taste the salt of the ocean on your lips. If your mind begins to wander, gently bring it back with compassion. You are not thinking, everything is simple, you are just being in the here and now; time doesn't matter, you simply are peacefully feeling, sensing, being, observing.*

As you become like your chosen sea creature, feel how you are a unique living being. Each of the creatures in the tide pools has a different color—you might be red, green, orange, brown, or purple. If you were a certain color, which one might it be right now? You each have different shapes as well … feel the general shape of your body, as if someone much bigger than you were to just look down and admire you. Some of you might feel smooth and flat; others might feel tightly curled and spiky. Each of you has a particular way of living and being in this environment … all of you make valuable contributions to the community. The other creatures rely on you in some way—maybe to bring nourishment, oxygen, protection, peace, helpfulness, or contentment. … Consider all the different creatures we have in the room with us—the presence of all the other beings around us makes this community richer and fuller, and makes life as we know it possible. … Without even one member, the entire community would change. Become aware of the creatures right next to you; without opening your eyes, try to sense something from the creatures/persons in front of or behind you … on your left or your right. Again, without using your eyes, can you detect something in them, something about their presence, their energy, their minds? Try to sense something about each person immediately beside you. Are you detecting peace, quietness, joy, hyper energy, needing to move, or something else? It's all okay; you are just observing and accepting them as they are, right this second. As we know, we all change regularly and we have our own secret reasons to do so. With this acceptance, allow yourself to be filled with a sense of connectedness to those around you, and gratitude for the unique roles you each play in your community. I will count down from 5, and when I have reached 1, we will all open our eyes. 5, 4, 3, 2, 1. Moving just your head, you can now look quietly at who's around you.

Discussion Questions

- *How are you feeling in your body right now?*
- *What was it like to not think?*
- *How many of you sensed something from the people around you? What did you sense from them?*
- *Did you feel a part of something bigger than you, a community? Why was that a good feeling, do you have any ideas? Sometimes it's hard to explain that feeling, but it's nice to try!*
- *What did you like about the creature you chose to be? When feeling like that creature, was there a special moment for you, a moment you'd like to remember?*
- *Did you discover something new about your body?*

Summary

What a beautiful and unique tide pool you all made! Our communities—in schools and workplaces or with family and friends—function similarly to tide pools. Each person is unique and contributes to the community in a specific way. This week, create moments when you are not thinking, and just be in the flow. Trust that

Figure 7.2. A Beautiful Meadow Scene Can Emerge Just from Our Minds.

others play a valuable role in your community even if it is not visible, and practice gratitude for what they provide.

Youth Variation

The tide pool does not require any variations.

Exotic Meadow

Words of wisdom: "Happiness is a butterfly, which, when pursued, is always just beyond your grasp; but which, if you will sit down quietly, may come and alight upon you."—Nathaniel Hawthorne

Intention: Become attuned to the rhythm of change within each community and how these changes help the community thrive.

Time: 20–30 minutes

Props: Photos of meadows throughout the seasons, as well as photos of different insects, trees, and flowers that live in meadows, such as lupines and daisies.

Overview

Participants are invited to notice certain aspects of meadows and embody different forms of life.

Facilitation

Today we will do an experiment with meadows, and how the different life-forms in the environment are changing all the time. How many of you remember visiting a meadow, maybe when you were hiking in the mountains or going to a picnic in a park? You may not have realized it, but meadows are a very important part of our world. Meadows act like giant, underground water reserves—they soak up water like a sponge and filter sediment from the water so that it's safe for the surrounding wildlife to drink. This life-giving environment allows both plant and animal life to flourish at an astonishing rate. Did you know that in Yosemite National Park in California, only 3% of the land is considered a meadow, but the meadows hold about one-third of the plant life species in the entire park?

The plant life in meadows is like a bouquet of beautiful colors (show photos of the meadow flowers). *Notice the details of these flowers. How are they similar, and how are they different? As many of you know, the wildflowers of the meadow usually bloom in the spring and summer. In the fall, the flowers fade, and the surrounding trees might shed their leaves in order to prepare for winter. The cold season brings snow that forms a tightly packed blanket on top of the meadow. As the weather gets warmer, the snow begins to melt, flooding the meadow. This influx of nutrients kicks off the growing season, and the cycle begins again* (show photos of seasons as you describe them). *The grass is the first thing to grow during this season—it can go from seed to flower in a matter of days! This grass supports the animals that live in this area. The meadow is full of small insects, such as grasshoppers and butterflies. These attract many other animals, including salamanders, frogs, and squirrels. Even deer and gophers may visit to graze on the grass. This small piece of land supports an abundance of life.*

We are now going to connect with the nature that fills the meadow. First, let's take a moment to bring awareness to our body. Close your eyes gently. Breathe in deeply through your nose and exhale through your mouth. Now breathe in deeply through your nose and exhale through your nose. Again … in nose … out mouth … in nose … out nose. Sense that your breath creates a gentle breeze around your nose. Now feel the weight of your body on the Earth. … Take another deep breath in, feeling the air fill your lungs. … Breathe out, exhaling the molecules your body no longer needs but may be used by other life-forms around you, like trees. … As you continue to breathe at a steady pace, your body might start to feel heavier. You may begin to hear sounds that you had tuned out, such as the rustling of the trees outside or birds singing (use relevant examples).

Imagine that you are a creature in a meadow. You might be a beautiful flower, a buzzing insect, a blade of grass, or a tall tree. If you choose to be a flower, you might feel your shoulders coming down and back, or your body opening up like a bud that is blooming. ... As a blade of grass, you may begin to sit up straighter, stretching your neck, reaching for the life-giving sunlight. ... If you have embodied a tree, you could feel rooted to the ground below you, solidly grounded like nothing could move you. ... How are you feeling different in your body when you become a meadow dweller? ... Feel the air around you shaping you more and more into a living being resting peacefully under the sky.

As you are relaxing in the experience of a meadow dweller, become aware of all the living beings amassed around you. ... Some are very tall, while others are short. ... Some are wide, and others are skinny. ... Some wear bright colors, whereas others tend to be dull or faded. ... Some tend to move a lot, easily swayed by the movement of air, water, wind, or the open space. ... Some tend to be fairly still no matter what happens around them, pushing their roots deep into the earth. ... Sense the presence of others around you, hear their breath, feel their energy level, their presence, their movement, if any. ... If your mind starts to wander, bring it back gently.

No matter their physical appearance, they are all valuable, making contributions that allow this ecosystem or community to survive storms, unexpected visitors, or difficult seasons. Every creature belongs here, adapting to the changing world around them. Each living being changes every day, ever so slowly, even in unpredictable ways. ... Change is often the only thing that is guaranteed in life. ... Often we don't notice it because we are so busy with other things, but when we pay close and careful attention, we notice the signs. It can be a slight color difference, a slight movement, an absence of a habit, an effort, or a slight wrinkle.

As the seasons change, we change with them. As summer turns to fall, the meadow dwellers prepare for a time of quiet, with spare sunlight and resources. ... How does your chosen meadow dweller prepare for the coming winter? If you are a tree, you might shed your leaves, leaving your body feeling lighter. ... If you are a flower or a blade of grass, you might feel your body shrinking back, leaving only a seed. ... Winter arrives, and snow covers the earth. You might feel heavier, sensing the weight of this ice blanket. ... From the outside, the meadow can look lifeless. Underneath, however, life is still there, waiting for the right time to reemerge. ... The sun returns, as it always does, to warm up the earth and melt the snow. The grass begins to grow, flowers bloom again, and the insects return. The meadow might enter a period when it explodes with life. ... How are you feeling the season your body is in right now? Do you feel the air differences, cold, warmth, droplets of water in the air?

Much like the meadow, our inner lives go through seasons. ... There is a time for growth, and a time for rest. ... There is a time for busyness, and a time for quiet. ... We shift and bend to the rhythm of life, adapting with resilience to the expected and unexpected changes. ... What is the season inside of you right now? ... Does it match the season outside? ... Is it a time of expansion and growth for you, when you are exposed to stimulating new experiences, or a time when your body will heal or recoup quietly? ... There are some changes we like, and others we do not, but change can be simply accepted and not judged as good or bad; it just is. We are all changing all the time. People changing and being different from one another is what allows us to find more solutions to problems when something arises. ... Sometimes things need to be repeated, and sometimes they do not ... since change is unavoidable, it is best to recognize, be respectfully curious, appreciate, and be patient with what is, as it is this exact way only for a while.

We will soon end this experience. If we are all ever so slightly different between when we started this mindfulness exercise and now, in which way are you different? ... Do you feel more peaceful, quieter? ... Do you have more energy? ... In which way might the others around you be different? ... Maybe someone is usually full of energy and feels really quiet now; maybe someone who is usually shy feels really strong and solid right now. ... Sometimes being beside someone feels like being beside a rock or a tree, deeply still. ... Just sense the presence of others around you. ... Take a final deep breath in, and out again. ... When you are ready, open your eyes.

Discussion Questions

- *What did you like about being a meadow dweller? Which being did you choose to be?*
- *Did you discover that your body can feel a certain way that it had not before, like having never been so still or not knowing you could actually not think and just be present?*
- *Did you feel a change between the beginning and the end of the experience? What's it like to actually be still enough to notice change happening? Which changes happened inside of you? Which changes happened in the room? With people around you?*
- *What do you think about the idea that everything is always changing? Has anyone noticed how each holiday or birthday is always different each year?*
- *If we were to tweak how we live because change is unavoidable, how should we be different? Should we appreciate more? Accept more? Be more patient with people?*

Summary

This week, attempt to stay focused on the present, and on being internally a beautiful and peaceful meadow creature. Notice the subtle changes that occur with each passing moment without judgment. There will never be another now.

Youth Variation
No variation necessary.

A Journey through Evolution

Words of wisdom: In letting go of imagining what could be better, "maybe we can realize that something very special is already occurring, and is always occurring, namely life."—Jon Kabat-Zinn

Intention: Experience the different life of other beings in a way that generates empathy and gratefulness for our own human existence.

Props: N/A for adults. For youth, images that make evolution somewhat visible such as sea creatures (for example a sea cucumber) and quiet mammals (such as koalas, sloths, sleeping deer). Recordings of ocean, forest, and city sounds can add a special touch to this experience.

Time: 20–30 minutes

Overview
Participants progress through different stages of evolution from a sea creature to a mammal to a human being.

Facilitation
I'd like to invite you into an embodiment experiment. As mentioned before, entering the world of different creatures allows us to embody certain mental states that we would be unlikely to discover otherwise. This is similar to actors practicing certain roles and emotions that stretch their experiences into something unfamiliar. We will challenge ourselves to shift through different forms of life. Start by settling in your body … and breathe, … allowing it to become heavier. … At your own pace, slow down your breath. … Take notice of your body,… which parts are long or short, … what's bulging, … what's moving with your breath versus remaining still. … If you were to see yourself from a great distance, in a faint light, and in water, could your shape be mistaken for an immobile sea creature? … Imagine yourself morphing into this sea creature, … a breathing, … peaceful being. … Imagine yourself becoming a sea creature of your choice and embody its shape fully. … Breathe like it, … feel its weight, … feel the air or water around it, … and moving ever so slightly. … Feel your mind settling into a non-thinking state of being,… just being and living. There are no thoughts … you are unable to think. … Feel the absence of time … just the present moment matters … feel detachment infiltrating your being. You are safe … and fed … and resting … and all is well.

... Take in the joy of just being, feeling grateful for the peaceful moment. ... Take a few breaths in this state of contentment, at your own pace, in the present time.

Now imagine evolution happened overnight (or a form of rebirth), and you woke up as a quiet elusive mammal on the land. What would be the first thing you'd notice? (Take a real pause here) *... Would you notice arms or legs ... or fur ... or a different head? Would you feel heavier? Would your skin feel different with the air around it? ... What would your body be like? It could be anything like a koala, sloth, mouse, sleeping deer, or any other creature.*

What is it like to wake up with such a different body? What kind of feeling arises? Does it trigger attentiveness ... focus ... or joy ... or something else? ... Notice that you are remaining still, but now it is by choice, as you have the possibility of moving. ... You are the same inside, heart and mind, embodying peace and contentment. ... Just being, interconnected with your environment, attuned to every motion around you but not alarmed, just sensing. ... Your ears are picking up sounds. ... Your nose is detecting scents. ... Your eyes, whether open or closed, can perceive light. ... Your mouth has a taste and level of humidity. ... Your skin or hide is feeling the air move. ... Become aware of your skin;... it has hair now as all mammals do, and it provides an extensive interface between you and the world around. ... All of this active sensing takes place in a state of perfect stillness. ... Fully embody your mammal of choice, becoming one with your perception of its experience ... feeling grateful for having access to all this rich sensory information. ... You are still peaceful and content, but your mind offers a rich experience of endless sensations. ... Take a few breaths in this state of contentment, at your own pace, in the present time. If your mind wanders, gently bring it back.

Now imagine evolution, or reincarnation, happened overnight again, and you wake up as a human being. ... What would your body feel like being, a child, teenager, adult, elder, someone of a different race or gender? ... Embody a human being of your choice. ... Be that person fully, the way you are holding your body, breathing, your facial expression, your breath, posture. ... Be aware of the arms and legs you own, of your fingers and toes, the head over your neck, the ability to later stand and walk on two legs, the sensation of clothes on your body, the floor that supports you and that was built by another human. ... Be aware of belonging to this group, to a family, a community of likeminded people. What emotion would you like to feel about waking up as this human being? ... Do many feelings coexist? ... If there were gratefulness for some aspects of this human experience, what would it be about? ... Dwell on an experience of gratefulness, see if you can inflate it, and fill each of your cells with it. ... Take a few breaths in this state of contentment, at your own pace, in the present time .... In a few seconds, I will count backward from 5 to 1, and we will all open our eyes, refreshed, ready to share and discuss our shape-shifting adventures. 5, 4, 3, 2, 1.

Discussion Questions

- *What was it like to be a sea creature? What stood out in your experience? Which sea creature did you choose? How would you describe the state of being you achieved? If there was a little something new in this state, what would that be?*
- *What was it like to be reborn into a mammal? Was there some loss, some gain? What stood out in terms of sensations? Was your presence different?*
- *What was it like to be transformed into a human being? Was there a mixture of emotions? Who did you choose to become? Is this a person you know or an imagined person? Did you experience any gratefulness?*

Summary

Reflecting on and embodying the experience of others—even different animals—can help us have a different perspective on ours and others' lives. This week, I encourage you to continue feeling grateful for your body and life even if it has limitations. As Jon Kabat-Zinn says, in letting go of imagining what could be better, "maybe we can realize that something very special is already occurring."

Youth Variation

The youth version can include a longer introduction with specific images of creatures and a discussion of their abilities and features. Hearing soft recordings of sounds from different environments can also make a big difference in helping youth transition from oceans to forests, and finally, to cities.

Sun Warming

Words of wisdom: When it comes to mindfulness, most animals have a lot to teach us.

Intention: Learn lessons of peace and relaxation from animals.

Time: 20–30 minutes

Props: Ideally, ask participants to bring a photo of a cat, dog, or horse they have loved. If possible, the animal should be in a sleeping position that can be somewhat mimicked. Alternatively, facilitators may also bring photos of various pets and animals sleeping (see Figure 7.3). Make sure to have one for each participant. Mammals are ideal because of their similarities with humans (we are mammals too!). Yoga mats and cushions are helpful, and small blankets can add a nice comfortable touch to the relaxation.

Figure 7.3. A Happy, Peaceful Cat Soaking Up the Sun.

Overview

The facilitator will collect a list of descriptive characteristics of pets or other mammals sleeping. It is important to write the characteristics on the board to start eliciting memories of these animals and their associated sensations.

Facilitation

Today is a pet day! Let's go around and you can each tell us three sentences about a pet you have cherished, a favorite animal, or the image you have chosen from my stack. Include his/her name if applicable, what you love about him/her, and how he/she inspires you. We have these furry visitors on our virtual team today. Who would like to start?

It was great meeting all these pets. Now let's list some of their attributes on the board when they are sleeping or relaxing. What do their bodies look like? What do you sense from them? Notice the position of their legs, heads, ears, eyes, breath, abdomen, and heartbeat. Also, take notice of their colors, the layout of their fur, where it's thinner, thicker, softer, and smoother. Close your eyes for a moment, and see if you can recreate the details of this photo in your mind … if an area is fuzzy, open your eyes and check for the missing information, and then close your eyes again to see if your mental image is now complete.

Now put the photo down at a safe place, and settle down on the floor or your chair, if possible in a position similar to your chosen sleeping animal. We will start our mindfulness exercise. At a particular moment, we will do a special breathing exercise, a type of sound with our mouth closed, but only three times. So you'll have to pay close attention to not miss the cue.

Close your eyes and visualize your chosen animal in your mind. Imagine that you are snuggled right beside him or her … your body is in a similar position, you're both sleeping or relaxing, and if that feels pleasant to you, imagine basking in the sun—it's not too hot; it's just right. … Most animals like to bask in the sun here and there and relax. … Cats' and dogs' body temperatures are slightly warmer than humans'. Feel the comfortable warmth in your body, the lethargy you and your animal are experiencing. Snuggle together. You are of the same kind and have a lot in common. … Feel your head heavily resting on the soft surface of your "fur"—i.e. your own hair covering your head, insulating it and keeping it warm. … Imagine sensing the fine "vellus" hairs in your face. We all have a lot of them; they are just so thin and pale that they are nearly invisible (they are less than 2 mm long!), but our face definitely has this subtle cover, similar to peach fuzz.

Now feel how your nose is sticking out, similar to most animals … your mouth is moist, and your jawbones are powerful. … Pay attention to all the sound surrounding you with your keen ears; smell the scent in the air, and see how many scents you can detect (many dogs can detect a 100 more than us). … You are both breathing the same air, sharing its nourishing qualities, inflating your lungs slowly and rhythmically. … Know you are safe. … Imagine a sense of togetherness with this animal and lose yourself in the comfort of a warm presence. … Nothing else in the world matters at this moment. You can just BE. … Feel your breath and your animal's rhythm; imagine you are breathing, in and out together, slowly, peacefully. … Feel a peaceful, loyal, trusting love that involves both of you. … Embody the qualities of the resting animal (use the list created with participants earlier). … *If your mind begins to wander, gently bring it back.*

As you lose yourself in the warm presence of your furry friend, take notice that many other living creatures are around you. … There are always living creatures around you, whether feathery birds, flying freely in the sky above, tiny ants marching determinedly on the cement around us, peaceful trees growing slowly but surely toward the sky, and buzzing insects like flies, butterflies, and bumblebees. … You are never truly alone on this Earth.

Option: *In a few seconds, we will take three breaths and with our mouth closed, exhale humming as if we were purring like a cat or expressing a sigh of satisfaction. Let's do it together without opening our eyes. First, take a deep breath and exhale gently purring or humming, noticing the relaxing vibration in your throat. It's like a throat massage. Do this again two times. Now become very quiet again and notice how still it feels inside. … You can get back to sleeping in the sun quietly again.*

Again, no matter where you are and what you do, you are never alone on this Earth. … The fragile pulses of life surround us. … There is always other life somewhere, someone who is basking in the sun or struggling with their own life challenge. … We can choose to connect virtually with the life force that inspires us most at this moment. ... Great peace can ensue from connection with nonhuman life; humans are most certainly the creature that struggles the most with letting go and resting fully into states of sleep and relaxation. ... We have much to learn from other creatures such as cats and dogs, who live mindfully to the best of their abilities, sleeping, loving, playing, and sensing. Notice how you are feeling now in your body. ... If there was something new in your state right now, what might it be? I will count backward from 3 to 1, and we will slowly find a comfortable seating position to discuss our experience. 3, 2, 1.

Discussion Questions

- *How many of you were able to recreate the presence of your animal?*
- *What were you able to feel? How did your body change? Did a part of your body in particular more easily become like your animal?*
- *Can anyone describe how their body feels different after connecting with their virtual animal? Did you discover something about relaxation?*
- *What did your senses notice? What kind of sound, smells, and warmth?*
- *Did your breathing pattern change? How was making a purring sound for you?*
- *What would you like to remember from this experience?*

Summary

In our society, busyness is prized. Most of us have lost touch with the ability to relax in the present moment like our pets and animals do. If you have pets at home, pay close attention to them this week—notice what they enjoy, what simple life pleasures fill their days. See if you can follow their lead for even 10 minutes during the day. If you do not have a pet, you can try to embody a friend's pet or an animal that inspires you.

Youth Variation

Very young children can bring a favorite stuffed animal or the facilitator can lend some. They can also bring a toy from their pet dog or cat, and have the object at hand to facilitate recall. There might be some hair on the dog or cat toy, a gentle reminder that is evocative of their pet. Children can be invited to lie down on their backs and put the stuffed animal on their neck or on their belly. If the toy is on their neck, you can pay careful attention to the soft touch of the "fur" on their faces or on their hands. Is there a different fabric to notice? If they position the stuffed animal or pet toy on their belly, they can pay attention to the lightness or the extra weight of it, the stability of the items on their navel, which part touches their clothes and which doesn't, and the movement of their abdomen.

Figure 7.4. Mountains Are a Natural Example of Quiet Power and Serenity.

Sierra Nevada Mountains

Words of wisdom: There are peaks of power in the depth of stillness.

Intention: Experience oneself as still, solid, and grounded.

Time: 20–30 minutes

Props: Photos of snowcapped mountains of different shapes (see Figure 7.4) and a broader view of the range they are located in; a whiteboard or big paper pad and markers. It is *crucial* for participants to sit either cross-legged on the floor or in chairs.

Overview

The facilitator encourages people to describe what they appreciate about mountains (solid, strong, immovable, powerful, impressive, etc.) and what mountains inspire in them (peacefulness, thoughtfulness, relaxation, patience, stillness, awe, etc.). This exercise will invite people first to feel stillness and awe by visualizing a mountain, and then to become one with the mountain by embodying qualities of "mountainness." This initial section is similar to Jon Kabat-Zinn's mountain meditation, except that we imagine here that some of the mountains have a very unique and precious area (which for adults is whatever is special to them, and for young people can be a mine of gemstones). Afterward, participants' awareness is shifted beyond their own state of "mountainness" into an acknowledgment of the existence of other mountains around them. The exercise ends with the realization of belonging to a group, a range, and being connected to others' wonderfulness. It is a powerful experience to become one of many titans in a mountain range. This conclusion gives a community flavor to the experience.

Facilitation

Today we will create an experience related to mountains. I have here a few photos of inspiring vistas. Raise your hand if you like mountains. Do you recognize some of these? Here's Everest, Rainier, Denali, etc. What do you like about mountains? Tell me which one of these photos is compelling to you and why. Let's write a list of mountain attributes on the board. ... When you have an opportunity to see a beautiful mountain, what effect does it have on you? (The facilitator writes these effects in another column on the board). *Those are great descriptions!*

Let's begin our exercise. Just to orient you, we will start by relaxing our bodies, and then everyone will connect with their own unique, internal image of their favorite mountain. It can be one from the photos we have admired, or an image you have in your own mind of another peak you've appreciated in the past. There are very specific shifts in the instructions for this exercise, so try to minimize the wandering of your mind as much as you can.

Start by sitting straight, with your feet flat on the floor if you are in a chair, and your hands on your lap. Take a deep breath through your nose and exhale slowly through your mouth. Do that again a few times, ... slowly, ... without forcing anything, ... and progressively slow down your exhale. ... On your next exhale, feel your body become a little more still and quieter. ... Take notice ... are all the different parts of your body slowing down at the same time? ... When you're ready, visualize in your mind your favorite mountain, or an image of a mountain, that you find beautiful and inspiring. ... Imagine that you are there admiring this mountain for its grandeur. ... See your mountain clearly, ... every detail of it, ... in your mind's eye. Is it peaceful, or are there lots of birds singing? ... Which colors adorn its different levels? ... Is the air cool or warm around it? ... Notice its solid base on the Earth, how does it connect to the Earth, in a steep or a gentle way? ... How different are the slopes around its frame? ... Are there areas that may be rocky ... or areas that are forested? ... See it in all its grandeur, in a three-dimensional way. ... Does it have a brook coming down one of its sides? ... Does it have a lofty peak, or two ... is it covered in snow?

When you see your mountain very clearly, ... bring the image of the mountain inside of you, ... as if a nature genie made you become one with this mountain. ... Your head becomes a mountain peak, and your seat becomes its solid base, rooted to the Earth. ... You and the mountain are one. ... You are the mountain, and you embody its grounded qualities of stillness. ... Feel the strength and power emanating from you. ... Feel the stillness and peace. ... How does it feel to be a mountain? ... Notice what happens inside of you, notice your head lifting toward the sky, the sense of solidity inside of you. ... Enjoy the sensations of feeling solid like rock. ... You are immovable, still, powerful (use the descriptors shared earlier), *regardless of what happens around you. ... If a snowstorm hits your mountain, it doesn't matter; you remain yourself, grounded. ... If a thick fog envelops you, or rain is pelting hard, or hail comes down, ... the mountain remains hard as rock, stable, not letting the outside world change the core of its existence. ... What happens on the outside stays on the surface. ... Even if a visiting tourist is disappointed by the appearance of the mountain, it doesn't change the mountain. ... The mountain remains itself. We have these qualities of "mountainness" inside of us, each one of us has a mountain of stillness, power, beauty, and peace inside. ... Each one of us can remain strong and solid inside, in spite of the different hardships that can happen outside of us. ... In fact, our inside can not only be as solid as a mountain but also contain undiscovered treasures or aspects that are particularly beautiful or valuable. ... If you'd like, locate what and where that might be on your mountain ... find a very special or precious spot ... feel it ... appreciate it. Hold the specialness of this spot in your mind's eye, and feel the grandeur of your mountain as a whole at the same time.*

As you are fully being your own unique mountain, expand your awareness to realize there are many other mountains around you. ... You are similar and different. ... You are connected and distinct; that balance is important—being with others yet not becoming them.... Without moving or opening your eyes, without judging if they're doing a good job, just feel the presence of others around you. ... Don't change anything in yourself, whether there's distraction or agitation around; just take notice. ... You are part of a bigger scene. See if you can sense the stillness, the strength, and the peace around you ... it is also okay if you don't feel it at this moment. ... Accept whatever there is, just as a mountain, without changing your state. ... Realize that everyone, every mountain, has beauty, calm, and stillness. ... You are part of a whole, and each mountain is unique. Some are smaller, some are bigger, some are easy to discover, others are much harder to discern, some have a lot of scars and others are pristine. ... They can look different on the outside, but inside, they are all made of the same substance. Their variations are what give a mountain range such a beautiful, unique, and distinctive appearance. ... Just as no two mountain ranges are identical, no two communities are identical, and this is yours to appreciate. I will count backward from 3 to 1, and at 1 you may all open your eyes. 3, take a deep slow breath; 2, feel how solid, grounded, and calm you are; 1, keep those qualities with you and open your eyes peacefully.

Discussion Questions

- *How many of you succeeded in feeling like a mountain?*
- *What was it like to feel a mountain inside of you? How did that change your body?*
- *Does anyone want to share what kind of mountain they were?*

- *What kind of special spot did you discover, where was it in your body, and how did it feel? If it paralleled a quality you have or an aspect of you that few people know about, what might it be?*
- *What about the storms, how was it to receive storms without flinching? Do you think we could do this in life as well? When?*
- *People are often surprised to discover how solid, strong, and confident they can be as a mountain. How many of you were surprised?*
- *How did you succeed in being part of a mountain range and sensing others (it's okay if you didn't)? What became different once you saw yourself as part of a range?*
- *What do you want to remember from the state of mountainness?*

Summary
We have much to learn from mountains—they are grounded, calm, and powerful. They are precious for many people and may store hidden secrets in their depths. Most of all, they will not be moved by the changing circumstances of life—they are always present. This week, try to practice being still and grounded no matter what happens, just like a mountain.

Youth Variation
With young people, it is fun to insert some gemstone and add the sentence: "*Some people believe that every mountain has an undiscovered streak of gold, silver, or other precious gemstone.*" The facilitator may consider bringing rocks and minerals to nourish participants' imaginations and help them experience colors, hardness, shininess, weight, etc. If possible, youth can be allowed to touch some of these items and feel how hard and solid they are, unyielding, heavy, powerful, and yet beautiful. They can feel the edges, weight, and softness of stones in their hands.

A Profound Human Challenge

Words of wisdom: Staying connected with an ocean of information can prevent us from drowning in a cold, shallow current. Peace is in the big picture.

Intention: Test our abilities to use all the strategies discussed in this program in the face of a human challenge: the sound of a child suffering.

Time: 30–40 minutes

Props: A 1-minute recording of a baby crying. Choose one that is not too heart-wrenching or angry; we want the exercise to be successful. In case of doubt, tone it down. Yoga mats, chairs, and a whiteboard are also helpful.

Overview

Participants are informed that this is "challenge day"! After allowing a few minutes for participants to settle in their favorite practice, the facilitator plays a recording of a baby crying. Participants are encouraged to anchor their experience in inner peace and avoid drifting into a negative emotional space.

Facilitation

This is the last day of our nature mindfulness series! You will have the opportunity to test your skills while listening to a recording of an unsettling sound. Most of you will be surprised by how far you have come with managing your emotions and keeping your own inner peace while still remaining aware of others. First, let's review what you have learned. What are some of the strategies you wish to remember from each of the exercises? (The facilitator writes the strategies on the board.)... *Let's start with the first exercise. Who would like to share what they remember and what was useful in the dot art, and being a pebble, exercise? ... How about the second exercise? ...* (The facilitator reviews each exercise and writes everyone's ideas on the board, adding any that may have been forgotten). *These strategies are like anchors into inner peace.*

We will now start our mindfulness exercise. You can choose to be seated or lie down on a mat. Whatever posture is most conducive to you centering yourself is ideal.

Find a comfortable position that you can hold for 30 minutes, one that does not require any effort. Allow all the lingering tensions from the day to melt away, especially if this was a busy day. ... Take a satisfying, deep breath in, and exhale slowly. ... Do that one more time, sensing the delicious air go through your nose, ... into your throat, ... and down into your lungs, ... fully inflating them with fresh oxygen from the trees,... nourishing and reenergizing every single cell in your body. ... Attempt to notice the scents in the air as all mammals do, ... and connect yourself to the center of your being ... and the world around you. Start with noticing parts of your body ... find some stillness within ... using some of your favorite strategies. ... Use the next few moments of silence to anchor yourself in your own center of stillness, like the eye of a tornado, where there is no movement even if the world around is spinning with busyness and sounds.

(1 minute of silence)

If your mind has wandered away, gently bring it back to your present focus, grounding yourself in inner peace by focusing on your breath, the ultimate link between life and death, our internal and external worlds, movement and stillness, filled and empty, sound and silence.

(about 1 minute of silence)

If your mind has wandered away, gently bring it back to your present focus, grounding yourself in inner peace by focusing on the sensations in your body, perhaps using a metaphor to guide your experience.

(about 1 minute of silence)

If your mind has wandered away, gently bring it back to your present focus, grounding yourself in inner peace by noticing your wholeness as a being and sensing the world around it, ... feeling the air brush against your skin, ... noticing the various sounds that appear and disappear around us, ... feeling the brightness of the light, ... and sensing other people around you. ... Notice all that is peaceful and still around you; ... sounds and silence coexist. ... Many other beings are near you yet separate from you, ... similar to you yet different. ... Feel your own, grounded body amidst these other lives. ... Take in the presence of all and everything that is still and peaceful. ... In a few seconds, I will introduce a recording of a voice that is not still and peaceful. ... I will introduce it lightly at first, and then will slowly increase the volume, without ever reaching a very loud level. ... Ground yourself in your own peace and in the peace you can find in those around you, as this will just be one voice amongst many others. ... You can choose how much space it will take in your consciousness. ... You can observe the emotions that arise in you without succumbing to them; ... just observe and take notice. ... I will count backward from 3 to 1 and start the sound. 3, 2, 1.

(Facilitator starts playing the recording of a crying baby at a very low volume, increasing it one notch after 10–15 seconds, but never blasting it too loud. We want the exercise to be successful and participants to experience themselves as capable. The ideal outcome is for participants to feel empowered and realize that they can control their emotions, and be connected to but not destabilized by others' emotions. The facilitator can notice participants' facial expressions, and if people look like they are struggling, either reduce the volume or encourage people to be a mountain, an ocean, or meadow of "groundedness.") *Suffering and difficulty happen to all living beings, but it is okay.... It is part of life, a part of growing, a part of the cycle of getting some needs met and not others. ... Try to experience love and compassion for the baby and people around the baby who may be doing the best they can to calm him/her. ... Be a soothing presence without drowning in the other's sadness or becoming annoyed by the sound. Choose your relation to the sound, ... being touched by it, having compassion for it, without making it your own. ... Your mind can stream different channels of information at the same time, just like having many windows open in your computer. ... You control the size of the window you are focusing on, ... and in which way you want to engage. ... Approach this sound in a kind, empathic way while protecting your integrity. ... The tears and sadness belong to him; they are in his body … you can maintain your own emotional temperature, so to speak, in your own body, even if you see another person in distress.*

I will stop the recording in a few seconds … (The facilitator stops the recording.) *Now take a few deep breaths in silence at your own pace. I will slowly count backward from 3 to 1, and we will all open our eyes. 3, 2, 1.*

Discussion Questions

- *How many of you had moments of feeling compassion for the child, without being captured by his or her emotions?*
- *What helped you do that? Which of the strategies we discussed were most important?*
- *What kind of person did you become?*
- *Does this state remind you of a person, a movie, a book, or an image?*
- *What was the hardest? Were you able to sustain that state throughout the 1 minute of crying, or did it fluctuate?*
- *Was any one thought particularly helpful? Did you remind yourself of something?*
- *Are you surprised you succeeded in doing this? What does that say about your abilities? What did you learn about yourself? What will you want to remember from this exercise?*

Summary

The sound of a baby crying is one of nature's most distressing sounds—we are wired to jump in, take the sadness on as our own, and make it stop! Today you all showed to yourselves that you can maintain your own calm and stillness inside, while still being connected to another's pain. You did this without losing yourself. This often requires a shift of perspective and a broader view. There is a great story of father and son that reflects this shift in perspective about suffering and privilege. Would you like to hear it? (See the end of Chapter 3). *Give yourselves a round of applause!*

Youth Variation

With young people, the sound of a baby crying may be annoying because of their experiences at home, such as jealousy, which could get in the way of accessing compassion. Most of them have not experienced the role of a caregiver, so a recording of a baby crying could have an effect different than intended. Depending on the age group, a recording of a dog and/or cat whining can be more effective with the majority of them. It is important to keep it at a lower volume and play it for a reduced amount of time: 20 seconds for children under 10 years old and 30–40 seconds for 10–16-year-olds. Discussion would include some of the following questions in addition to, or in lieu of, those mentioned above:

- *When is it important for young people to have compassion?*
- *Which adults have been models of compassion in your lives?*
- *How could schools better cultivate compassion?*
- *When do you wish adults expressed more compassion?*
- *What is a social cause that triggers compassion for you?*
- *Do you like being a compassionate person and why?*

CHAPTER EIGHT

Becoming Lords of the Rings

In the Lords of the Rings project, adults and youth discover that after practicing focusing and concentration skills, they can have control over another dimension of life: their temperature. People are progressively trained to warm up one hand *intentionally* through a series of creative mindfulness meditations. Mood rings, biodots, and other cost-effective biofeedback devices that dramatically change color when exposed to warmth are involved. These items provide exciting, visible, and concrete representations of people's mental influence over their bodies, leading to an increased sense of self-confidence, self-worth, and agency.

This project is intriguing for all ages and has been facilitated with beginners with no mindfulness experience, as well as experienced participants. The first session is written for beginners and can be skipped with experienced groups, or it can be enhanced with an advanced breathing exercise from Chapter 4. Adults have usually seen mood rings before but are interested by the idea of altering their own body temperature through a mental exercise. This project is best facilitated by instructors who are experienced mindfulness practitioners and truly capable of increasing warmth in their hands.

Amazing Possibilities and Choices

Words of wisdom: You cannot choose the *external* events that happen to you, but you can choose your *inner* experiences of all things.

Intention: Establishing a context of mystery and confidence in people's abilities.

Time: 20–30 minutes

Props: Photos of people walking on coals. A mood ring in a box or other biofeedback devices. Some adults may be more intrigued by more novel biofeedback devices, such as biodots or stress cards, than the well-known mood rings.

Overview

The facilitator provides examples of incredible feats people accomplish around the world, such as walking on coals, lying on a bed of nails, acrobatics, etc. to heighten people's interest. The idea of adjusting the temperature of one's hand is introduced, and its implications for intentionally changing the color of a mood ring just by concentrating. In this first visit, participants are invited to simply practice the skill of sitting still together in silence. As mentioned earlier, if this group has learned the other projects in this book, this first session can be skipped.

Facilitation

Thank you for being here today. I'm someone who is interested in the mind's extraordinary abilities. Some people in the world train their minds to handle very difficult things. For example, some people learn to walk on hot coals without burning their feet. Monks in the distant and snowy mountains of the Himalayas engage in competitions to see who can warm up the greatest number of wet, ice cold towels on their shoulders. Closer to us, just the other day, I was talking to someone who told me he had been stung by a wasp when walking barefoot on the beach. How many of you have been stung by a wasp? I have too, and it hurts, doesn't it? Since the stinger was still in his foot, he was faced with the daunting task of removing it, which seemed like it would hurt even more. So this person, with his powerful mind, decided to imagine his foot was a cloud so that it would hurt less when the stinger was pulled out. He closed his eyes, focused on his breath, and pretended that his foot was a soft cloud from which it was very easy to remove a stinger. It worked!! (Lower voice). *In fact, he barely felt the stinger going out. This person had trained his mind to be powerful so he could do that. You don't have control over what happens to you, but you have control over what happens in your mind.*

People have such powerful minds that they can actually change the color of mood rings at will, after just a little training. As many of you may know, a mood ring is made with a special kind of quartz that changes color when it is warmed up (show a ring in a box so that it remains at room temperature and doesn't change in front of their eyes right away). *It will change color on its own when it is left in the sun, but you can also learn to warm it up and change its color just with the power of your mind. I was wondering if you would be interested in learning this trick?*

Okay, the first step is to learn to breathe. The breath is a powerful tool in any mindfulness task we want to master. Sit up straight, uncross your legs, and place your feet on the ground if you can. Put your hands on your lap and close your eyes. You will focus your mind on breathing "air" in and out. I may ask you some questions. These are for you to find the answers in your own body and they are not to be answered out loud.

Start by focusing on the air that goes into your nose and the air that goes out. Imagine that it is a nice substance that goes into your nose and fills your head with calm and happiness. You are slowly breathing in fresh air, … like good feelings, … and enjoying. … You can imagine this nice substance will slowly go down a slide in the back of your throat and into your lungs. … This substance becomes the perfect temperature for your body and can be analgesic, like a soft pain-killer syrup, or medicinal, like a warming syrup when we're cold. … It can soothe your body very gently of everything—agitation, anxiety, hyper energy, worries, hurts, pain, discomfort, and upset feelings. It makes your belly feel full and relaxed. … Put your hands slowly on your lower belly and feel it moving because of this wonderful nourishing substance we call air. … Take a really deep and slow breath of fresh good feelings, without forcing. If your mind wanders away from what I'm saying, just kindly bring it back to focusing on your breathing in and out. Make sure you do it slowly and let as much air out as the amount that came in.

Now continue taking peaceful breaths, very slowly, without making sounds, and see if you can even get some air to go in both of your arms, one at a time. Choose one arm and send air down your shoulder, arm, wrist, hand, and fingers and see if any bubbles of tension, hyper energy, or discomfort need to be washed away. Your ability to clear and relax your arm will be very important when we work with the mood ring. Relax each finger one by one … finger 1 … 2 … 3 … 4 … 5 (the thumb counts as a finger!). *Do you feel a difference between the hand we observed and the one we didn't? Sometimes people feel lighter or heavier. Let's try the other arm as silently as we can, even slower than before. Slowly send air to your shoulder … elbow … wrist … hand … fingers, finger 1 … 2 … 3 … 4 … 5. Take a few seconds to notice that both hands are probably relaxed now, and see if they feel more relaxed than other parts of your body. I will count to 3 and when I get to 3, we can all open our eyes slowly and talk about what you noticed. 1, 2, 3. Wow! That was really quiet!*

Discussion Questions

For all discussions, these questions are simply a jumping-off point and a way to trigger curiosity. Feel free to choose what works best for your group, and remind them that these questions are just to help them reflect on the experience; we do not expect them to always have an answer right then and there.

- *How many of you enjoyed having a few minutes of quiet time like that? What was it like? Did anyone discover something about their body?*
- *Did anything distract anyone? If so, how did you keep your wandering mind from taking over?*
- *What difference does it make to know that you can do that? You did that so well I have no doubt you can all change the color of a mood ring. I think you'll be ready to start learning how to warm up your body next time.*

Summary

Remember this secret: you don't have control over the outside of you, but you always have some control over your experience of your body. Give yourselves a hand!

Youth Variation

Children are usually very excited and motivated to develop this ability, which seems magical. If the group is very young, the first step can be to tame "the wiggles and giggles" with deep breaths such as Tornado breaths in Chapter 4. Facilitators can say: "*Giggles and wiggles are a lot of fun, but let's see if you have the power to control them. Some people may have a hard time doing this because it takes lots of concentration, so make sure you just do your own best and ignore what happens with others.*" The time sitting still is often reduced with children, and their age is usually a good estimate of the number of minutes they can succeed in concentrating intently (e.g., 5 minutes for a 5-year-old).

Temperature Shifts

Words of wisdom: Wherever you are, wherever you go, your breath is with you and can offer comfort.

Intention: Notice sources of warmth in the body and develop the ability to access it.

Time: 20–30 minutes

Props: Mood ring in a box or ring stand (or other biofeedback devices).

Overview
The facilitator greets people with enthusiasm and asks them what they remember from what was talked about last time. Afterward, people are invited to notice the differences in temperature between:

- The air that goes in their nose versus the air that goes out;
- Their face and the air around them in the room;
- Their hands placed on their lap and their thighs.

The facilitator will again pay attention to the level of calm in the room and conclude the session when most participants are still successfully concentrating and before too many start to lose their focus.

Facilitation
Can someone volunteer to summarize what we talked about last week? Wonderful. Would anyone like to add to that great summary? (Take as many people's comments as possible, as this is an important way of connecting with participants and transitioning into the exercise.) *You folks remember a lot!*

We talked about the powers of the mind. Sometimes we can't control what happens to us, but we can control what our mind does with it. A breath can be calming and act as a peaceful substance to clear our body of upset feelings and unnecessary thoughts.

Today we will practice noticing temperature. It is important for you to notice where there is warmth in your body if you are to warm up a mood ring. I will also show you what color the ring can become when it is warm (walk around and show the box with the ring visible). *Tell me the current color of the ring* (show it, but do not allow people to touch it as some have very warm hands, which would change the color immediately and ruin the excitement for the exercise). *Okay, everyone saw that it is yellow* (some may be black or green; it's all fine). *I will make it change as we do the exercise. Is everybody ready?*

Let's start by putting our feet flat on the floor, closing our eyes, and taking a deep breath. I will ask you lots of questions, but just answer them in your own mind. These questions are to help you direct your attention, not to answer out loud. Take a few slow and silent breaths to clear your body of tensions and blow them out slowly. Now breathe normally and pay attention to the air coming into your nose. See if you can feel the difference in temperature between the air that goes in and the air that goes out. Continue taking more deep breaths and noticing the temperature differences or changes. As you breathe in slowly and quietly, see if you can feel more specifically where, in the air canal, does the air change temperature? … Is it when entering your nose, … inside your nose, … in your throat, … in your esophagus (i.e., the slide deep inside your neck), … or is it in your lungs? … Follow the air with your mind as your eyes would follow a leaf-boat on a river to see what happens to it. … If your mind wanders away, it's okay, just gently bring it back.

Now pay attention to your face. … Is the temperature of your face different from that of the air around you? … Sometimes you might even feel the air moving around your nose or cheeks; see if you can feel that. … The air around us often feels a little cooler than our body. … It's wonderful to realize how warm our body can be even if it's cold around us. … If your mind wanders away, it's okay, just gently bring it back

When you've felt the air temperature around you, let's see if you can breathe in and send air down your legs and notice temperature differences in your legs. Our body temperature is not the same everywhere. Different parts of the body are warmer. Let's start with one foot of your choice. … Check out what is the warmest spot in that area … your toes?… the bottom of your feet? … the top of your feet? … the side of your feet? … or your ankle? … Focus on that warmth. … How would you describe this warmth to an alien? … Would there be smoke, colors, a feeling of density? … What words would describe the warm area?… Can you draw a mental circle around the warm area and distinguish where the warmth begins and ends? … Now continue breathing slowly, keeping your attention on your breath and trying to observe the sensations in your leg. … Where is the warmest spot there? … Is it in your calf? … the front of your knee? … the back of your knee? … or your thigh? … Observe your leg carefully and find warmth. … Scan your leg for the warmest spot and again, try to see if you can draw a circle around it with your mind … imagine which color it is, and how you would describe it to an alien. … Some people think the inside of the knee is warmest, others their thighs, others another spot. Notice warmth. … If your mind wanders away, it's okay, just gently bring it back to one leg.

When you're ready, take another deep breath and switch your attention to your other leg. Take a deep breath and send the air all the way down to that second leg and foot. Now take a minute to compare your observations of this new leg with the sensations of the foot and leg you've just finished observing. Do you feel the difference between a body part you've focused your mind on and relaxed, versus a body part you haven't? … For many people, focusing and observing a body part makes it heavier … sometimes it also feels bigger and warmer. If you don't feel anything yet, that's okay.

Are the warmest spots the same in this second foot and leg? … Again, notice the warmest spots; if you are focusing on your foot, would it be in your toes… the bottom of your feet ... the top of your feet ... the side of your feet ... or your ankle? ... Scan your foot to find the warmest spot ... and when you find it, just pay close attention to how big it is and how it feels.

When you're ready, observe your leg itself and find the warmest spot. ... Would it be the top of your knee ... under your knee ... your thigh? Again, when you find it, try to describe it and draw a circle around its edges. If your mind wanders away, it's okay, just gently bring it back.

Now (pause to enhance their attention and allude to something special coming) *notice that your hands are positioned on your lap. Try to observe the difference between the temperature of your hands and the temperature of your lap. ... Which one is warmer and which one is colder? ... Does the position of your hands matter? ... Is it the same difference on both sides? ... Notice these sensations in both of your hands while still breathing deeply, in and out, slowly.*

When you're ready, see if you can take a deep breath of soothing air that will flow nicely over all of your body. I will count to 3 and then everyone will open their eyes and share their observations. 1, breathe deeply and slowly; 2; 3.

Okay, would you like to see the color of the mood ring now? (The facilitator keeps the ring or other biofeedback device in his/her own hand but shows it around). *It became blue because I increased the warmth in my hand. You will learn how to increase the warmth in your hand next time.* (See Figure 8.1).

Figure 8.1. Mindfulness Practices Can Teach Us How to Warm Our Bodies with the Power of Our Minds!

Discussion Questions

- *What was that like for you? What was the difference between the leg you focused on and the one you didn't?*
- *Did anyone discover warm spots? How would you describe a warm spot to an alien?*
- *Did anyone come up with colors for the warm spots?*
- *Did anyone notice that focusing on your breath is very calming and comfortable?*

Summary

The breath is generally seen as very calming, and the good news is that it is always there with you! Wherever you are, wherever you go, it's with you and can comfort you. Even someone who's put in jail or is having big problems has access to breathing to comfort him/herself. You all look very relaxed now. It was fun doing this exercise with you today. Give yourselves a hand!

Youth Variation

The facilitator can ask engaging questions such as: "*Do you still want to learn how to change the color of a mood ring?*" There is usually an enthusiastic response. If not, then pretend that you didn't hear anything, rub your ear, and ask again.

Tapping into Inner Power

Words of wisdom: You have the power to change the "inside" of you.

Intention: Introduce the concept of "moving sensations" and how people can change their inner experiences.

Time: 20–30 minutes

Props: N/A

Overview

Concepts such as soothing power of breath, ability to notice the various temperatures in our body, and our access to calm are reviewed through participants' comments. When people have been given enough time to share, the day's practice is introduced: with concentration, we can actually *change* what is going on in our bodies. For example, some experienced meditators can reduce allergy sniffles, stop a hiccup, or soothe a hurting belly.

Facilitation

What do you remember from last week? Has anyone used these ideas on their own? What difference did it make? Has anyone noticed their breath even just one time? Do you remember how we talked about the powers of the mind, and how sometimes we can't control what happens to us but we can control what our mind does with it? Today we will practice what the mind can really do. You will actually change something in your body! Have you ever noticed how focusing on pain makes it bigger? We can use the power of focusing on other sensations to alter their size in useful ways.

Start by putting your feet flat on the floor, closing your eyes, and taking a deep breath. As usual, I will ask you lots of questions, but I want you to answer in your own mind only. These questions are just to help you direct your attention, not to answer out loud. Take a few slow and silent breaths to clear your body of tensions. Inhale slowly and exhale (facilitator does this as well). *Think of where tensions may be hidden and blow them out slowly without making any sounds. … Make sure you send some air all the way down to your toes. Let's try this one more time silently and slowly. The more silent and slow, the more powerful you are.*

Now breathe normally and pay attention to your body: what is warm… what is cold? Let's try to find the coldest spot in your body. Start by scanning one foot and leg (repeat slowly), *then scan the other foot and leg* (repeat slowly). *If your mind wanders away, it's okay, just gently bring it back. Then scan a hand and its arm; you are still trying to find the coldest spot in your body* (repeat). … *Now scan your other hand and arm* (repeat). … *Are your toes or your hands colder? … Continue to breathe slowly and deeply. … Now scan your face and see if there is a cold spot there. … Pay attention to your nose, cheeks, and ears and see if they are cold. … Any cold spot anywhere in your body can work, but the most common are toes, fingers, and nose.*

Choose a cold spot you'd like to warm up. If your mind wanders away, it's okay, just gently bring it back to choosing a spot you'd like to work on. … If you can't find a cold spot, that's okay, choose a finger or a toe to warm just to practice the exercise. Once you've decided on a spot, see if you can locate a warm feeling somewhere near it. Locate a sensation of warmth close to the cold spot and focus intensely on the warmth. … Very slowly try to feel it more, … find the center of the warmth, … imagine how deep it is, … see if it has a color, … pretend it is like a sun that is heating you up. … Feel this warmth vibrating. … Some people feel a beat or a pulsation in the warmth. … Notice that the warmth is growing slowly and even expanding a little as you are focusing on it. … Allow it to seep like warm water and progressively touch the areas around it. … See if you can make the warmth progressively reach the cold spot and fill it up slowly. … You may feel the warmth taking over that part of your body, or simply become mixed somehow with the cold. … Just focus on your own unique sensations and play with the power of your mind to change your body temperature at that spot. If your mind wanders away, it's okay, just gently bring it back to the warmth, and enjoy it, appreciate its presence and how lucky you are to have that glowing warmth available to you. ... Sometimes discovering that we can play with the warm feelings in our body makes us smile lightly and be pleased with ourselves. ... Allow yourself to be satisfied with what your mind can do, whether it accomplished a big or a little change. For many people, it feels good to have some control over our sensations.

We will soon end this exercise. Continue feeling the warmth and the appreciation, and think about how you would describe your experience. ... I will slowly count backward from 3 to 1 and after that we will all open our eyes and talk about the experience. Take a deep breath that fills all of your body slowly and silently with comfort and contentment. 3, 2, 1. Open your eyes.

Discussion Questions

- *How many of you were able to change your body temperature a little? Wonderful!*
- *How many of you changed the temperature of your toes? Your fingers? Your nose?*
- *Who would like to share how it went or what it was like? Which colors came to your mind?*
- *What did you imagine the warmth was?*
- *Was anyone surprised by what they accomplished? What does it mean that you accomplished this? Can it be a helpful skill? When might you use this?*

Summary

Today we explored the powers of your mind to change how your body feels just by noticing parts that are feeling good and concentrating on expanding the comfortable feeling. Most of you were successful. There are some days when we are better at it than others. If we're hungry or didn't sleep enough, sometimes it's a little harder to concentrate, but with practice I know you can all achieve this.

Youth Variation

None necessary for this session except the usual: ask enthusiastic questions and involve young people in sharing their experiences.

Focused Attention Allows Transformation

Words of wisdom: Focused attention allows transformation.

Intention: Practice attentive focusing on a body part and warming up one hand.

Time: 20–30 minutes

Props: Mood ring

Overview

After a review, the facilitator announces that participants are now ready to do the mood ring pretest. The mood ring pretest will consist of actually warming up one hand of their choice in its entirety. They will keep the hand warm in complete silence for 1 minute. Participants are usually excited by this announcement, which also offers the opportunity to discuss, later on, how even in the midst of excitement they can successfully calm their minds and focus.

The exercise starts as usual by clearing tensions in the body, and then building up warmth in the entire hand. Participants have to practice generating enough heat so that it will warm not only their hands but also an object like the ring. When the hand is completely warmed up, people are invited to contrast it with their other hand. Most people will find a significant temperature difference and become excited by this previously unknown ability.

Facilitation

Raise your hand if you remember what we talked about last week. Wonderful! Who would like to share what you remember? Yes, we talked about our power to transform experiences inside of us. Has anyone attempted to transform an experience of their bodies? What are the different discomforts we can transform using these ideas? What can you transform discomfort into?

Today we will practice building up enough heat in our hand that we can warm up not only our hand but also an object outside of it. This is the skill of intensifying or increasing sensations that we want. We will also practice sustaining this heat in our hand for 1 minute or more because it takes a little time for the mood ring to change color. The mood ring will change color either with gentle warmth over time or with high intensity in a short time. I will instruct you to close your hand at some point. It is best to not tighten your muscles. As you probably know, there is less blood flow in a tight hand (demonstrate) *and we need more blood if we want the hand to be warm. So try to keep it relaxed like this* (demonstrate a relaxed, loosely closed hand).

Start with your feet flat on the floor, and your hands on your lap. Take a few slow and silent breaths to clear your body of tensions. Inhale slowly and exhale silently (facilitator does this as well). *Feel the air coming into your nose and traveling down your body, bringing fresh oxygen to all your cells and cleaning your body of all tensions. Make sure you send some air all the way down to your toes. Let's try this one more time silently and slowly. The more silent and slow, the more powerful you are. If your mind wanders away, it's okay, just gently bring it back.*

Now breathe normally and send some fresh air down the arm you'd like to focus on today, all the way to your hand. Focus on the center of your palm and get in touch with the sensations there. You might feel something like a heartbeat. Your hand is "alive," it is made of living cells that accomplish a lot for you everyday. Take a moment to feel grateful for all that this hand allows you to do; you are lucky to have it. Now slowly, as slowly as you can so that a person watching you may not even notice, close your hand softly. ... Locate the warmth in the middle of your hand and see how it feels. ... For some people it can almost feel like the warm fur of a cuddly little animal, for others it may feel like warm sand. ... See what comes to your mind if I say the warmth is like ... . Finish the sentence in your head. ... Focus on it and imagine it growing and filling the space of your gently closed hand. ... Feel the warmth maybe slowly expanding into your fingers and maybe even forming a warm mitten, or maybe not. It is all fine; just experience whatever is happening in your hand with interest and curiosity. Feel the vibration that comes with the warmth. ...Enjoy the sensation of peace and comfort that radiates from this hand.

For a brief moment, check out the temperature in your other hand and see if you feel a difference between the one you worked on and the one you didn't. ... Then bring your attention back slowly to the one you've been working on. ... Put a number to the warmth on a scale of 1 to 5 ... now on your next inhale, imagine you can increase this warmth one notch. Enjoy the warmth in your hand.

Now expand your awareness from the warm hand to the air around it, maybe your hand is radiating heat, like a little sun. ... Notice that the air around you is also very silent, even though many of you are sitting here today.... What do you appreciate about this silence? How does it feel to be part of a group focused on the same activity and peacefully doing their best?

As I mentioned earlier, part of this pretest is to see if you can hold this warmth in your hand in complete silence for 1 minute (and maybe even longer). Continue focusing on the warmth and on being as still, silent, and appreciative as possible. We will now begin our time of silence.

(1 minute of silence)

I will do a countdown for five deep breaths, and after that we will open our eyes. Imagine that your entire body is a balloon and that each in-breath fills up your nose and head and then goes down to your abdomen and arms and legs. 5, continue breathing slowly, in and out (pause); 4, take another slow breath, inhale, exhale, and notice how relaxed your entire body might feel (pause); 3, let the air in and out, some of you may even feel a little heavier because you are very relaxed (pause); 2, some of you may feel warm and calm and are preparing yourself to come back to the room, quietly (pause) … last breath inhale … and exhale; 1, you can now open your eyes and feel refreshed as if you had taken a nice nap.

Discussion Questions

- *What was it like? Did you succeed in warming your hand?*
- *Which part of the exercise was most helpful in you affecting the warmth of your hand?*
- *What images came to your mind?*
- *What difference did it make to keep your hand warm with a group of silent people doing the same thing around you?*

Summary

Focused attention allows transformation. We also discovered that this group can be incredibly silent and concentrate with great power. Next week is your mood ring test. I will give each one of you a mood ring (that you can keep!) to practice using the power of your mind. Give yourselves a hand!

Youth Variation

More emphasis can be placed on the value of silence when concentrating on a task, if relevant.

The Temperature Test

Words of wisdom: If you can change your body, you can change how you feel.

Time: 20–30 minutes

Props: Enough mood rings or biofeedback items for every participant.

Overview

Participants are looking forward to testing their ability to change the mood ring (see Figure 8.2). Hopefully this is not an overly hot day when the mood rings or biofeedback devices are already in the blue tones. A review including a list of strategies is written on a big paper pad or board. The box of mood rings is shown without being touched so people can see which color they are before the meditation begins. Participants are then instructed to place one hand facing up and the other one facing down so that we know which hand is to receive the ring (the one open face up). Once settled in a position, with the ring, they can begin warming up their hand first and extending the

Figure 8.2. Are You Ready to Change the Color of Your Ring?

warmth into the ring. The facilitator will talk slowly and progressively direct them to move from the breath, to focusing on sending air down the arm, to finding warmth in the center of their hands, and allowing it to expand and encompass the ring.

Facilitation

Let's list on the board all the strategies we have discussed in this project. … I think you are all definitely ready to do the mood ring test! (Show the rings in a box). *Let's notice which color they are right now when we are not touching them.*

Let me first explain how we will do the exercise. You will start as usual by putting your feet flat on the floor, closing your eyes, placing your hands on your lap, and taking a deep breath. You will place one hand facing down like this (demonstrate) *and one hand facing up like this* (demonstrate). *When everyone seems ready, I will walk around and place a mood ring in the hand that is open. In this way you get to choose which hand you want to work with today. When you receive the ring, you will keep your eyes closed and just focus on feeling the ring in the palm of your hand and trying to warm it up using all the tricks we have explored. Is everyone ready?*

Okay, place your feet flat on the floor if you can, put your hands in your lap, position one hand to receive the ring, and close your eyes. Take a few slow and silent breaths to clear tensions. … The more relaxed your body is, the warmer and more comfortable your hands become. … Inhale slowly and exhale silently (facilitator does this as well). *Feel the air coming into your nose and traveling down your body, bringing fresh oxygen to all your cells and clearing your body of all tensions. … Think of where tension may be hidden and blow it out slowly without making any sounds. Make sure you send some air all the way down to your toes. … Let's try this one more time silently and slowly. The more silent and slow, the more powerful you are. If your mind wanders away, it's okay, just gently bring it back. Continue breathing slowly, keeping your body still and your eyes closed, while I walk around and place a ring in your hand. … When you receive it, close your fingers on it softly and examine it only by touching, without looking, just with your fingers. … Feel the original temperature of the ring. … Is it cold or room temperature? … Feel the weight of the ring. Is it heavy or light?… Feel the texture and notice any difference between the texture of the inner material versus the external coating. … How would you describe the difference? … Are they equally soft?*

Now leave the ring in the palm of your hand, but close your fingers on it as if it was an egg nested into a little pouch. … Do not hold on tightly or tense up your hand muscles;… just relax your hand softly on the ring. … Continue breathing deeply and focusing on the warmth filling up your hand and fingers. (Very slowly, the facilitator directs people into using each of the strategies listed on the board as possibilities to become increasingly calm and warm up the ring).

Imagine this ring becoming part of your hand. … Imagine it is softly becoming integrated in your palm. … Don't move it, just feel it. … What images come to your mind? … Some people feel it's like a flower tattooed on their hand or a fire. … What images come to you as you allow the ring to become the same temperature of your hand and sink into your skin? … If your mind wanders away, it's okay, just gently bring it back.

Now sit still in complete silence with the ring for 1 or 2 minutes. … I will now count backward slowly from 5 to 1 and when you open your eyes, you can look at your ring and show it to your neighbors. 5, 4, 3, 2, 1. Open your eyes.

Discussion Questions

- *How did it go? How many of you changed the color of the ring?*
- *Which strategy worked best for each one of you?*
- *Did you know you could be that powerful? Did you know you could calm yourself down so much so that it actually changes your body?*
- *What was it like to have an object in your hand? What images came to your mind?*
- *When you see this mood ring from now on, can it remind you of something about yourself?*
- *How can this learning apply to your life and to managing different emotions and challenges?*

Summary

You have learned that your mind is very powerful! It can change the temperature and transform feelings in your body! Congratulations on developing the power of your mind. Give yourselves a hand!

Youth Variation

Young people become very enthusiastic about this session. This creates an opportunity to highlight how we can calm ourselves successfully even when something very exciting happens. The facilitation is similar except that they are told that the ring will be given only once we see that they are being perfectly still and really meditating. This is easily visible by the amount of eye movement and tension in the facial muscles. A discussion of how they will avoid losing the ring is also recommended: "*You will each get one of those and you'll have to be careful not to lose it because I do not have more than one per person. What might be a good place to put the mood rings so that people do not lose them? I have some strings here too if someone wants to tie it around your wrist as a bracelet or at the end of the string as a necklace.* Depending on the age group, if the children tend to be rowdy, it may be worth planning to go outside after the session so that they can celebrate and share.

References

Anderson, B. A. (2013). A value-driven mechanism of attentional selection. *Journal of Vision, 13*(3), 7–7. https://doi.org/10.1167/13.3.7.

Atkinson, B. J. (2013). Mindfulness training and the cultivation of secure, satisfying couple relationships. *Couple and Family Psychology: Research and Practice, 2*(2), 73–94. https://doi.org/10.1037/cfp0000002.

Barnes, S., Brown, K. W., Krusemark, E., Campbell, W. K., & Rogge, R. D. (2007). The role of mindfulness in romantic relationship satisfaction and responses to relationship stress. *Journal of Marital and Family Therapy, 33*(4), 482–500. https://doi.org/10.1111/j.1752-0606.2007.00033.x.

Barrett, C. J. (2017). Mindfulness and rehabilitation: Teaching yoga and meditation to young men in an alternative to incarceration program. *International Journal of Offender Therapy and Comparative Criminology, 61*(15), 1719–1738. doi: 10.1177/0306624X16633667.

Beaudoin, M. N. (2010). *The SKiLL-ionaire in every child: Boosting children's socio-emotional skills using the latest in brain research.* San Francisco, CA: Goshawk Publications.

Beaudoin, M. N. (2013). *Bullies to buddies: From problem management to developing ALL children's social and emotional skills [Video].* United States: Alexander Street Press Videos.

Beaudoin, M. N. (2014). *Boosting ALL children's social and emotional brain power: Life transforming activities.* Thousand Oaks, CA: Corwin Press Publications.

Beaudoin, M. N. (Fall, 2018). Thinkitis vs. Mindfulness. *Family Therapy Magazine*, AAMFT, September–October, 36–40.

Beaudoin, M. N., & Duvall, J. (2017). *Collaborative therapy and neurobiology: Evolving practices in action.* New York: Routledge, Taylor & Francis.

Beaudoin, M. N., & Taylor, M. (2009). *Responding to the culture of bullying and disrespect: New perspectives on collaboration, compassion and responsibility* (2nd ed.). Thousand Oaks, CA: Corwin Press Publications.

Beaudoin, M. N., & Walden, S. (1998). *Working with groups to enhance relationships*. Duluth, MN: Whole Person Associates Publisher.

Beaudoin, M. N., Moersch, M., & Schnare, B. (2016). The effectiveness of narrative therapy with social and emotional skills development: An empirical study of 835 children's stories. *Journal of Systemic Therapies*, *35*(3), 42–60.

Bellezza, S., Paharia, N., & Keinan, A. (2017). Conspicuous consumption of time: When busyness and lack of leisure time become a status symbol. *Journal of Consumer Research*, *44*, 118–138. doi:10.1093/jcr/ucw076.

Benson, H., Lehmann, J. W., Malhotra, M. S., Goldman, R. F., Hopkins, J., & Epstein, M. D. (1982). Body temperature changes during the practice of g Tum-mo yoga. *Nature*, *295*(5846), 234–236. doi: 10.1038/295234a0.

Brandsma, R. (2017). *The mindfulness teaching guide: Essential skills & competencies for teaching mindfulness-based interventions*. Oakland, CA: New Harbinger Publications.

Bruya, B., & Tang, Y. Y. (2018). Is attention really effort? Revisiting Daniel Kahneman's influential 1973 book *Attention and Effort*. *Frontiers in Psychology*, 9, 1133. https://doi.org/10.3389/fpsyg.2018.01133.

Carey, B. (2019). "Screen time" is over. *New York Times*. Retrieved from www.nytimes.com/2019/05/31/health/screen-time-mental-health-screenome.html

Castro, J. (2014). Gasp! 11 surprising facts about the respiratory system. In *Live Science*. Retrieved from www.livescience.com/44105-respiratory-system-surprising-facts.html

Chen, L. H., Wu, C.-H., & Chang, J.-H. (2017). Gratitude and athletes' life satisfaction: The moderating role of mindfulness. *Journal of Happiness Studies*, *18*(4), 1147–1159. https://doi.org/10.1007/s10902-016-9764-7.

Chow, D. (2013). Why humans are bad at multitasking. *Live Science*. Retrieved from www.livescience.com/37420-multitasking-brain-psychology.html

Chun, M. M., Golomb, J. D., & Turk-Browne, N. B. (2011). A taxonomy of external and internal attention. *Annual Review of Psychology*, *62*(1), 73–101. https://doi.org/10.1146/annurev.psych.093008.100427.

Cooper, C. D., Kong, D. T., & Crossley, C. D. (2018). Leader humor as an interpersonal resource: Integrating three theoretical perspectives. *Academy of Management Journal*, *61*(2), 769–796. https://doi.org/10.5465/amj.2014.0358.

Costandi, M. (2014). Brainy processing at your fingertips. *The Guardian*. Retrieved from www.theguardian.com/science/neurophilosophy/2014/sep/08/brainy-processing-at-your-fingertips

Davidson, R. J., Kabat-Zinn, J., Schumacher, J., Rosenkranz, M., Muller, D., Santorelli, S. F., ... Sheridan, J. F. (2003). Alterations in brain and immune function produced by mindfulness meditation. *Psychosomatic Medicine*, 65(4), 564–570. https://doi.org/10.1097/01.PSY.0000077505.67574.E3.

Day, M. A., Jensen, M. P., Ehde, D. M., & Thorn, B. E. (2014). Toward a theoretical model for mindfulness-based pain management. *Journal of Pain*, *15*(7), 691–703. https://doi.org/10.1016/j.jpain.2014.03.003.

Dhillon, A., Sparkes, E., & Duarte, R. V. (2017). Mindfulness-based interventions during pregnancy: A systematic review and meta-analysis. *Mindfulness*, 8, 1421–1437. doi: 10.1007/s12671-017-0726-x.

Diamond, A. (2013). Executive functions. *Annual Review of Psychology*, 64, 135–168. doi: 10.1146/annurev-psych-113011-143750.

Duncan, L., Cohn, M., Chao, M., Cook, J., Riccobono, J., & Bardacke, N. (2014). Mind in labor: Effects of mind/body training on childbirth appraisals and pain medication use during labor. *Journal of Alternative and Complementary Medicine*, *20*(5), A17. doi: 10.1089/acm.2014.5040.abstract.

Farb, N. A. S., Segal, Z. V., Mayberg, H., Bean, J., McKeon, D., Fatima, Z., & Anderson, A. K. (2007). Attending to the present: Mindfulness meditation reveals distinct neural modes of self-reference. *Social Cognitive and Affective Neuroscience*, *2*(4), 313–322. https://doi.org/10.1093/scan/nsm030.

Feldman, C., & Kornfield, J. (1991). *Stories of the spirit, stories of the heart: Parables of the spiritual path from around the world*. San Francisco, CA: Harper San Francisco.

Fiske, S. (2018). *Social beings: Core motives in social psychology* (4th ed.). Hoboken, NJ: John Wiley & Sons.

Fissler, M., Winnebeck, E., Schroeter, T., Gummersbach, M., Huntenburg, J. M., Gaertner, M., & Barnhofer, T. (2016). An investigation of the effects of brief mindfulness training on self-reported interoceptive awareness, the ability to decenter, and their role in the reduction of depressive symptoms. *Mindfulness*, *7*(5), 1170–1181. https://doi.org/10.1007/s12671-016-0559-z.

Frank, C., & Schack, T. (2017). The representation of motor (inter)action, states of action, and learning: Three perspectives on motor learning by way of imagery and execution. *Frontiers in Psychology*, 8, 678. doi: 10.3389/fpsyg.2017.00678.

Froh, J. J., Bono, G., & Emmons, R. (2010). Being grateful is beyond good manners: Gratitude and motivation to contribute to society among early adolescents. *Motivation and Emotion*, 34(2), 144–157. https://doi.org/10.1007/s11031-010-9163-z.

Gard, T., Taquet, M., Dixit, R., Hözel, B. K., de Montjoye, Y., Brach, N., … Lazar, S. W. (2014). Fluid intelligence and brain functional organization in aging yoga and meditation practitioners. *Frontiers in Aging Neuroscience*, 6(76), 1–12. doi: 10.3389/fnagi.2014.00076.

Geiger, M. J., Neufang, S., Stein, D. J., & Domschke, K. (2014). Arousal and the attentional network in panic disorder. *Human Psychopharmacology: Clinical and Experimental*, *29*(6), 599–603. https://doi.org/10.1002/hup.2436.

Germer, C. K. (2014). *The mindful path to self-compassion: Freeing yourself from destructive thoughts and emotions*. Kbh.: Nota.

Gorman, T., & Gree, C. (2016). Short-term mindfulness intervention reduces the negative attentional effects associated with heavy media multitasking. *Scientific Reports*, 6, 24542.

Gottlieb, J., Oudeyer, P. Y., Lopes, M., & Baranes, A. (2013). Information-seeking, curiosity, and attention: Computational and neural mechanisms. *Trends in Cognitive Sciences*, *17*(11), 585–593. https://doi.org/10.1016/j.tics.2013.09.001.

Guendelman, S., Medeiros, S., & Rampes, H. (2017). Mindfulness and emotion regulation: Insights from neurobiological, psychological and clinical studies. *Frontiers in Psychology*, 8(220), 1–23. doi: 10.3389/fpsyg.2017.00220.

Hagen, S. (2012). The mind's eye. University of Rochester. Retrieved from www.rochester.edu/pr/Review/V74N4/0402_brainscience.html

Hansen, G. R., & Streltzer, J. (2005). The psychology of pain. *Emergency Medicine Clinics of North America*, *23*(2), 339–348. https://doi.org/10.1016/j.emc.2004.12.005.

Hanson, R., & Mendius, R. (2009). *Buddha's brain: The practical neuroscience of happiness, love & wisdom*. Oakland, CA: New Harbinger Publications.

Harbaugh, C. N., & Vasey, M. W. (2014). When do people benefit from gratitude practice? *Journal of Positive Psychology*, 9(6), 535–546. https://doi.org/10.1080/17439760.2014.927905.

Harris, S. (2014). *Waking up: A guide to spirituality without religion*. New York: Simon & Schuster.

Hölzel, B. K., Carmody, J., Vangel, M., Congleton, C., Yerramsetti, S. M., Gard, T., & Lazar, S. W. (2011). Mindfulness practice leads to increases in regional brain gray matter density. *Psychiatry Research*, *191*(1), 36–43. doi:10.1016/j.pscychresns.2010.08.006.

Howard, M. W., & Kahana, M. J. (1999). Contextual variability and serial position effects in free recall. *Journal of Experimental Psychology: Learning, Memory, and Cognition*, 25(4), 923–941. doi: 10.1037/0278-7393.25.4.923.

Irwin, D. E. (2001). Eye movements and perception. In Smelser, N. J., & Baltes, P. B. (Eds.), *International encyclopedia of the social & behavioral sciences* (pp. 5208–5210). Oxford, England: Elsevier.

Jacoboni, M. (2009). *Mirroring people: The science of empathy and how we connect with others*. New York: Picador.

Jensen, E. (2008). *Brain-based learning: The new paradigm of teaching*. Thousand Oaks, CA: Corwin Publishers.

Jha, A. P., Stanley, E. A., Kiyonaga, A., Wong, L., & Gelfand, L. (2010). Examining the protective effects of mindfulness training on working memory capacity and affective experience. *Emotion*, *10*(1), 54–64. doi: 10.1037/a0018438.

Kabat-Zinn, J. (1990). *Full catastrophe living: Using the wisdom of your body and mind*. New York: DELTA.

Kabat-Zinn, J. (2004). *Wherever you go, there you are*. London: Piatkus.

Kabat-Zinn, J. (2005). *Coming to our senses: Healing ourselves and the world through mindfulness*. New York: Hyperion.

Kabat-Zinn, J. (2015). Mindfulness. *Mindfulness*, 6(6), 1481–1483. https://doi.org/10.1007/s12671-015-0456-x.

Kahneman, D. (2011). *Thinking, fast and slow*. New York: Farrar, Straus and Giroux.

Kakigi, R., Nakata, H., Inui, K., Hiroe, N., Nagata, O., Honda, M., … Kawakami, M. (2005). Intracerebral pain processing in a yoga master who claims not to feel pain during meditation. *European Journal of Pain*, 9(5), 581–589. doi: 10.1016/j.ejpain.2004.12.006.

Kashdan, T. B., Afram, A., Brown, K. W., Birnbeck, M., & Drvoshanov, M. (2011). Curiosity enhances the role of mindfulness in reducing defensive responses to existential threat. *Personality and Individual Differences*, 50(8), 1227–1232. https://doi.org/10.1016/j.paid.2011.02.015.

Keyworth, C., Knopp, J., Roughley, K., Dickens, C., Bold, S., & Coventry, P. (2014). A mixed-methods pilot study of the acceptability and effectiveness of a brief meditation and mindfulness intervention for people with diabetes and coronary heart disease. *Behavioral Medicine*, 40(2), 53–64. https://doi.org/10.1080/08964289.2013.834865.

Khaddouma, A., Gordon, K. C., & Bolden, J. (2015). Zen and the art of dating: Mindfulness, differentiation of self, and satisfaction in dating relationships. *Couple and Family Psychology: Research and Practice*, 4 (1), 1–13. doi: 10.1037/cfp0000035.

Kornfield, J. (1993). *A path with heart: A guide through perils and promises of spiritual life* New York: Bantam Books.

Kozhevnikov, M., Elliott, J., Shephard, J., & Gramann, K. (2013). Neurocognitive and somatic components of temperature increases during g-Tummo meditation: Legend and reality. *PLoS ONE*, 8(3), e58244. https://doi.org/10.1371/journal.pone.0058244.

Kral, T. R., Schuyler, B. S., Mumford, J. A., Rosenkranz, M. A., Lutz, A., & Davidson, R. J. (2018). Impact of short- and long-term mindfulness meditation training on amygdala reactivity to emotional stimuli. *NeuroImage*, 181, 301–313. doi: 10.1016/j.neuroimage.2018.07.013.

Kushlev, K., & Dunn, E. W. (2015). Checking email less frequently reduces stress. *Computers in Human Behavior*, 43, 220–228. https://doi.org/10.1016/j.chb.2014.11.005.

Lahnakoski, J. M., Glerean, E., Jääskeläinen, I. P., Hyönä, J., Hari, R., Sams, M., & Nummenmaa, L. (2014). Synchronous brain activity across individuals underlies shared psychological perspectives. *NeuroImage*, *100*, 316–324. https://doi.org/10.1016/j.neuroimage.2014.06.022.

Lazar, S. W., Kerr, C. E., Wasserman, R. H., Gray, J. R., Greve, D. N., Treadway, M. T. … Fischl, B. (2005). Meditation experience is associated with increased cortical thickness. *Neuroreport*, *16*(17), 1893–1897.

Li, J., Long, L., Liu, Y., He, W., & Li, M. (2016). Effects of a mindfulness-based intervention on fertility quality of life and pregnancy rates among women subjected to first in vitro fertilization treatment. *Behaviour Research and Therapy*, *77*, 96–104. https://doi.org/10.1016/j.brat.2015.12.010.

Loh, K. K., & Kanai, R. (2014). Higher media multi-tasking activity is associated with smaller grey-matter density in the anterior cingulate cortex. *PLoS ONE*, 9(9), e106698. doi: 10.1371/journal.pone.0106698.

Lorenz, J., Hauck, M., Paur, R. C., Nakamura, Y., Zimmerman, R., Bromm, B., et al. (2005). Cortical correlates of false expectations during pain intensity judgment: A possible manifestation of placebo/nocebo cognitions. *Brain, Behavior, and Immunity*, *19* (4) 283–295.

Luders, E., Cherbuin, N., & Gaser, C. (2016). Estimating brain age using high-resolution pattern recognition: Younger brains in long-term meditation practitioners. *NeuroImage*, *134*, 508–513. doi: 10.1016/j.neuroimage.2016.04.007.

Lutz, J., Brühl, A. B., Doerig, N., Scheerer, H., Achermann, R., Weibel, A., … Herwig, U. (2016). Altered processing of self-related emotional stimuli in mindfulness meditators. *NeuroImage*, *124*, 958–967. https://doi.org/10.1016/j.neuroimage.2015.09.057.

Lutz, J., Brühl, A. B., Scheerer, H., Jäncke, L., & Herwig, U. (2016). Neural correlates of mindful self-awareness in mindfulness meditators and meditation-naïve subjects revisited. *Biological Psychology*, *119*, 21–30. https://doi.org/10.1016/j.biopsycho.2016.06.010.

Majeed, M. H., Ali, A. A., & Sudak, D. M. (2018). Mindfulness-based interventions for chronic pain: Evidence and applications. *Asian Journal of Psychiatry*, *32*, 79–83. https://doi.org/10.1016/j.ajp.2017.11.025.

Martín-Perpiña, M., Poch, F. V., & Cerrato, S. M. (2019). Media multitasking impact in homework, executive function and academic performance in Spanish adolescents. *Psicothema*, *31*(1), 81–87. doi: 10.7334/psicothema2018.178.

McRae, K., Misra, S., Prasad, A. K., Pereira, S. C., & Gross, J. J. (2012). Bottom-up and top-down emotion generation: Implications for emotion regulation. *Social Cognitive and Affective Neuroscience*, *7*, 253–262. doi: 10.1093/scan/nsq103.

Miodrag, N., Lense, M. D., & Dykens, E. M. (2013). A pilot study of mindfulness intervention for individuals with Williams syndrome: Physiological outcomes. *Mindfulness*, *4*, 137–147. doi: 10.1007/s12671-012-0178-2.

Monti, D. A., Kash, K. M., Kunkel, E. J., Moss, A., Mathews, M., Brainard, G. … Newberg, A. B. (2013). Psychosocial benefits of a novel mindfulness intervention versus standard support in distressed women with breast cancer. *Psycho-Oncology*, *22*, 2565–2575. doi: 10.1002/pon.3320.

Neff, K. (2011). *Self-compassion: The proven power of being kind to yourself*. New York: William Morrow.

Nummenmaa, L., Glerean, E., Viinikainen, M., Jaaskelainen, I. P., Hari, R., & Sams, M. (2012). Emotions promote social interaction by synchronizing brain activity across individuals. *Proceedings of the National Academy of Sciences*, *109*(24), 9599–9604. https://doi.org/10.1073/pnas.1206095109.

Nummenmaa, L., Saarimäki, H., Glerean, E., Gotsopoulos, A., Jääskeläinen, I. P., Hari, R., & Sams, M. (2014). Emotional speech synchronizes brains across listeners and engages large-scale dynamic brain networks. *NeuroImage*, *102*, 498–509. https://doi.org/10.1016/j.neuroimage.2014.07.063.

Paolini, C. (2005). *Eldest*. New York: Alfred A. Knopf.

Pathak, N. (2017). Fun facts about your hands. *WebMD*. Retreived from www.webmd.com/osteoarthritis/rm-quiz-handfacts

Peacock, C. E., Hayes, T. R., & Henderson, J. M. (2019). Meaning guides attention during scene viewing, even when it is irrelevant. *Attention, Perception, & Psychophysics, 81*(1), 20–34. https://doi.org/10.3758/s13414-018-1607-7.

Pinheiro, A. P., Barros, C., Dias, M., & Kotz, S. A. (2017). Laughter catches attention! *Biological Psychology, 130*, 11–21. doi: 10.1016/j.biopsycho.2017.09.012.

Plude, D. J., Enns, J. T., & Brodeur, D. (1994). The development of selective attention: A life-span overview. *Acta Psychologica*, 86(2–3), 227–272. https://doi.org/10.1016/0001-6918(94)90004-3.

Prakash, M., & Johnny, J. C. (2015). What's special in a child's larynx? *Journal of Pharmacy & Bioallied Sciences, 7*(1), S55–S58. doi: 10.4103/0975-7406.155797.

Ralph, B. C., Thomson, D. R., Cheyne, J. A., & Smilek, D. (2014). Media multitasking and failures of attention in everyday life. *Psychology Research, 78*(5), 661–669. doi: 10.1007/s00426-013-0523-7.

Reck, S. G., & Hund, A. M. (2011). Sustained attention and age predict inhibitory control during early childhood. *Journal of Experimental Child Psychology, 108*(3), 504–512. https://doi.org/10.1016/j.jecp.2010.07.010.

Ribeiro, M. (2017). 8 fun facts about lungs. In *Pulmonary Hypertension News*. Retrieved from https://pulmonaryhypertensionnews.com/2017/12/20/8-fun-facts-lungs/

Rodríguez-Carvajal, R., García-Rubio, C., Paniagua, D., García-Diex, G., & De Rivas, S. (2016). Modelo integrador de mindfulness (MIM): El cultivo de los estados mentales positivos hacia uno mismo y los demás a través del mindfulness y la autocompasión. *Anales de Psicología, 32*(3), 749. https://doi.org/10.6018/analesps.32.3.261681.

Rosenberg, M. D., Finn, E. S., Scheinost, D., Papademetris, X., Shen, X., Constable, R. T., & Chun, M. M. (2016). A neuromarker of sustained attention from whole-brain functional connectivity. *Nature Neuroscience, 19*(1), 165–171. https://doi.org/10.1038/nn.4179.

Russell-Williams, J., Jaroudi, W., Perich, T., Hoscheidt, S., El Haj, M., & Moustafa, A. A. (2018). Mindfulness and meditation: Treating cognitive impairment and reducing stress in dementia. *Reviews in the Neurosciences, 29*(7), 791–804. doi: 10.1515/revneuro-2017-0066.

Salomons, T. V., Nusslock, R., Detloff, A., Johnstone, T., & Davidson, R. J. (2015). Neural emotion regulation circuitry underlying anxiolytic effects of perceived control over pain. *Journal of Cognitive Neuroscience, 27*(2), 222–233. https://doi.org/10.1162/jocn_a_00702.

Salzberg, S. (2010). *The force of kindness: Change your life with love and compassion*. Boulder, CO: Sounds True.

Sänger, J., Bechtold, L., Schoofs, D., Blaszkewicz, M., & Wascher, E. (2014). The influence of acute stress on attention mechanisms and its electrophysiological correlates. *Frontiers in Behavioral Neuroscience*, 8(353), 1–13. doi: 10.3389/fnbeh.2014.00353.

Savage, B. M., Lujan, H. L., Thipparthi, R. R., & DiCarlo, S. E. (2017). Humor, laughter, learning and health! A brief review. *Advanced Physiological Education*, 41(3), 341–347. doi: 10.1152/advan.00030.2017.

Schutte, N. S., & Malouff, J. M. (2018). Mindfulness and connectedness to nature: A meta-analytic investigation. *Personality and Individual Differences*, 127, 10–14. https://doi.org/10.1016/j.paid.2018.01.034.

Shapiro, S. L., & Carlson, L. E. (2010). *The art and science of mindfulness: Integrating mindfulness into psychology and the helping professions*. Washington, DC: American Psychological Association.

Shin, M., Webb, A., & Kemps, E. (2019). Media multitasking, impulsivity and dual task ability. *Computers in Human Behavior*, *92*, 160–168. doi: 10.1016/j.chb.2018.11.018.

Singleton, O., Hözel, B. K., Vangel, M., Brach, N., Carmody, J., & Lazar, S. W. (2014). Change in brainstem gray matter concentration following a mindfulness-based intervention is correlated with improvement in psychological well-being. *Frontiers in Human Neuroscience*, 8(33), 1–7. doi: 10.3389/fnhum.2014.00033.

Smalley, S. L., & Winston, D. (2010). *Fully present: The science, art, and practice of mindfulness*. Cambridge, MA: Da Capo Lifelong.

Solano López, A. L. (2018). Effectiveness of the mindfulness-based stress reduction program on blood pressure: A systematic review of literature. *Worldviews on Evidence-Based Nursing*, *15*(5), 344–352. https://doi.org/10.1111/wvn.12319.

Spanne, A. (2015). 14 funky facts about feet. In *Mental Floss*. Retrieved from http://mentalfloss.com/article/72021/14-funky-facts-about-feet

Spinhoven, P., Huijbers, M. J., Zheng, Y., Ormel, J., & Speckens, A. E. M. (2017). Mindfulness facets and big five personality facets in persons with recurrent depression in remission. *Personality and Individual Differences*, 110, 109–114. https://doi.org/10.1016/j.paid.2017.01.045.

Stahl, B., & Goldstein, E. (2010). *A mindfulness-based stress reduction workbook*. Oakland, CA: New Harbinger Publications.

Strick, M., Holland, R. W., Van Baaren, R., & Van Knippenberg, A. (2010). Humor in the eye tracker: Attention capture and distraction from context cues. *Journal of General Psychology*, *137*, 37–48.

Sullivan, B., & Thompson, H. H. (2013). *The plateau effect: Getting from stuck to success*. New York: Dutton.

Sun, S., Hu, C., Pan, J., Liu, C., & Huang, M. (2019). Trait mindfulness is associated with the self-similarity of heart rate variability. *Frontiers in Psychology*, *10*, 314. https://doi.org/10.3389/fpsyg.2019.00314.

Sünbül, Z. A., & Güneri, O. Y. (2019). The relationship between mindfulness and resilience: The meditating role of self compassion and emotion regulation in a sample of underprivileged Turkish adolescents. *Personality and Individual Differences*, 139, 337–342. doi: 10.1016/j.paid.2018.12.009.

Tanaka, G. K., Maslahati, T., Gongora, M., Bittencourt, J., Lopez, L. C. S., Demarzo, M. M. P., ... Velasques, B. (2015). Effortless attention as a biomarker for experienced mindfulness practitioners. *PLOS ONE, 10*(10), e0138561. https://doi.org/10.1371/journal.pone.0138561.

Thich Nhat Hanh. (2015). *Silence: The power of quiet in a world full of noise*. New York: Harper Collins.

Tolle, E. (2004). *The power of now: A guide to spiritual enlightenment*. Vancouver: Namaste Publishing.

Vago, D. R., & Silbersweig, D. A. (2012). Self-awareness, self-regulation and self-transcendence (S-ART): A frameword for understanding the neurobiological mechanisms of mindfulness. *Frontiers in Human Neuroscience*, 6(296), 1–30. 10.3389/fnhum.2012.00296.

van der Kolk, B. A. (2014). *The body keeps the score*. New York: Penguin Books.

van der Schuur, W. A., Baumgartner, S. E., Sumter, S. R., & Valkenburg, P. M. (2015). The consequences of media multitasking for youth: A review. *Computer in Human Behavior*, 53, 204–215. 10.1016/j.chb.2015.06.035.

Voci, A., Veneziani, C. A., & Fuochi, G. (2019). Relating mindfulness, heartfulness, and psychological well-being: The role of self-compassion and gratitude. *Mindfulness, 10*(2), 339–351. https://doi.org/10.1007/s12671-018-0978-0.

Vygotsky, L. (1978). *Mind in society: The development of higher psychological processes*. Cambridge, MA: Harvard University Press.

Wang, J., Geng, L., Schultz, P. W., & Zhou, K. (2019). Mindfulness increases the belief in climate change: The mediating role of connectedness with nature. *Environment and Behavior, 51*(1), 3–23. https://doi.org/10.1177/0013916517738036.

Weitzberg, E., & Lundberg, J. O. (2002). Humming greatly increases nasal nitric oxide. *American Journal of Respiratory and Critical Care Medicine, 166*(2), 144–145. doi: 10.1164/rccm.200202-138BC.

White, M., & Epston, D. (1990). *Narrative means to therapeutic purposes*. New York: W. W. Norton & Company.

White, Michael. (2007). *Maps of narrative practice*. New York: W. W. Norton & Company, Inc.

Zeidan, F., Emerson, N. M., Farris, S. R., Ray, J. N., Jung, Y., McHaffie, J. G., & Coghill, R. C. (2015). Mindfulness meditation-based pain relief employs different neural mechanism than placebo and sham mindfulness meditation-induced analgesia. *Journal of Neuroscience, 35*(46), 15307–15325. doi: 10.1523/JNEUROSCI.2542-15.2015.

Zeidan, F., Johnson, S. K., Diamond, B. J., David, Z., & Goolkasian, P. (2010). Mindfulness meditation improves cognition: Evidence of brief mental training. *Consciousness and Cognition*, doi: 10.1016/j.concog.2010.03.014.

Zupan, Z., Blagrove, E., & Watson, D. G. (2018). Learning to ignore: The development of time-based visual attention in children. *Developmental Psychology*, 54(12), 2248–2264. https://doi.org/10.1037/dev0000582.

Index

About the Authors

Marie-Nathalie Beaudoin, PhD, is the founder of Skills for Kids, Parents, and Schools (SKIPS), which offers a variety of counseling services, creative mindfulness programs, socio-emotional skills projects, and collaborative therapy trainings in the San Francisco Bay Area. Marie-Nathalie's life was significantly changed after she involved herself fully in a Mindfulness-Based Stress Reduction program in the early 1990s, and thereafter attended numerous seminars with his Holiness the Dalai Lama, Thupten Jinpa, Jon Kabat-Zinn, Jack Kornfield, and Rick Hanson, to name only a few. She has also traveled in India, Nepal, and Tibet, where she thoroughly enjoyed learning from the rich and wise heritage of these cultures.

Beaudoin has been a pioneer in finding effective ways of combining mindfulness, collaborative therapies, and neurobiology in order to assist youth and adults in developing their potential and living a more satisfying life. She is the author of several books, including *Boosting ALL Children's Social and Emotional Brain Powers: Life Transforming Activities* (2014) and the popular *The SKiLL-ionaire in Every Child: Boosting Children's Socio-emotional Skills Using the Latest in Brain Research* (2010), written for parents, teachers, and therapists, and translated into French and Spanish (see www.skillionaire.org). More recently, she coedited *Collaborative Therapy and Neurobiology: Evolving Practices in Action* (2017), which describes some of her innovative practices with adults. Her work has been featured in a number of professional DVDs, and in magazines such as *Educational Leadership*, *Teaching Tolerance*, AAMFT's *Family Therapy*, and *The California Educator*.

With a background in improvisational theater, Marie-Nathalie is an acclaimed international speaker with frequent engagements in Canada, Europe, and South America, where she is renowned for her entertaining and thought-provoking presentations (www.mnbeaudoin.com).

Kelsey Maki received her BS in human development from Northwestern University and her MS in clinical psychology at the University of San Francisco. She is currently working toward her PsyD in clinical psychology at the University of San Francisco. Her primary clinical focus is developing social-emotional skills in children and families, and helping them use these skills to navigate adversity. Kelsey began facilitating groups in 2008, and has continued to lead various groups in her work and her clinical psychology training. She came to SKIPS during her graduate training, where she collaborated with Marie-Nathalie to deliver numerous mindfulness-based exercises in local schools. Kelsey enjoys incorporating mindfulness into many aspects of her work and life—she is fascinated by the way mindfulness enriches awareness and how physical and mental health are deeply interconnected.

Made in United States
North Haven, CT
04 November 2026

21726083R10113